I...
and...

By Nikolai Gogol

THE MARRIAGE
FROM A MADMAN'S DIARY
INSPECTOR
GAMBLERS

In versions for the English-language theatre

By Eric Bentley

with a preface and three appendices

APPLAUSE
THEATRE BOOK PUBLISHERS

The picture on the cover shows Alec Guinness as Hlestakov in INSPECTOR.

Library of Congress Cataloging-in-Publication Data

Gogol', Nikolai Vasil'evich, 1809–1852.
    Inspector and 3 other plays.

    The Marriage, Inspector and Gamblers are translated from the Russian; From a madman's diary is an adaptation of the short story, Zapiski sumasshedshego.
    Bibliography: p.
    Contents: The Marriage — From a madman's diary — Inspector — [etc.]
    1. Gogol', Nikolai Vasil'evich, 1809–1852—Translations, English. I. Bentley, Eric, 1916–   . II. Title. III. Title: Inspector and three other plays.
PG3333.A19   1987   891.72'3   86–28818
ISBN 0–936839–12–0 (pbk.)

Applause Theatre Book Publishers
211 W. 71st Street
New York, NY 10023
212-595-4735

First Applause Printing, 1987.
Second Applause Printing, 1992.

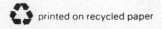 printed on recycled paper

ACKNOWLEDGMENTS

First acknowledgment should go to those who taught me what Russian I managed to learn: Franziska de Graaff and Konstantin Reichardt; second, to those who have helped out by knowing more Russian than I do: early on, this was chiefly Leon Stilman, my colleague at Columbia University; later, it was Simon Karlinsky, whom I have known only through his writings, in books and letters; third, I'd like to thank those who have performed these "versions." *Gamblers* began, in the Nineteen Fifties, at the HB Studio in New York. *The Marriage* has had various productions culminating, one might say, in a BBC-TV production with John Wood as Podkolyossin in the Eighties. I owe a special debt to the *belief* in all this work of my publisher Glenn Young of Applause Theatre Books.

E.B.   New York, January 1987

The comic is . . . the world of anarchy, not of order. It offers a complete alternative to the principled universe, opposes saturnalia to the faith, undermines with the pervasive secret religion of meaninglessness. The comic affirms that the everlasting powers are not the powers that be, but the perpetrators of orgy. But . . . the comic is not mere animal darkness. The animal is in conflict with a courageous, personal, poetic vision. Caught in this anomaly, many comic writers have suffered from melancholy and hypochondria . . . The purest example of the comic genius is Gogol.

— V.S. Pritchett

CONTENTS

PREFACE

with a chronology

A Gogol Chronology

1809:	born in Sorochintsy in the Ukraine
1821:	entered Nezhin High School
1828:	graduated there, left for St. Petersburg
1829:	began to publish (poetry)
	visited Germany
	got a Civil Service job in St. Petersburg
1830:	published stories
1831:	left the Civil Service, taught at a girls' school in St. Petersburg
	met Pushkin
	published Evenings on a Farm at Dikanka, Volume I
1832:	Evenings . . . Volume II
1834:	became Assistant Professor of World History at the University of St. Petersburg
1835:	Arabesques (a Gogol miscellany that includes three great stories: Nevsky Avenue, The Portrait, and A Madman's Diary)
	Mirgorod (two volumes of stories)
1836:	première of The Inspector General (May 1)
1836-48:	lived mostly abroad
1842:	Dead Souls
	The Overcoat
1847:	Selected Passages from Correspondence with Friends
1852:	died in Moscow

Though Gogol himself supervised the issue of a "Collected Works" in four volumes that appeared in 1842, many items appeared only posthumously. These include:
An Author's Confession
The Divine Liturgy of the Eastern Church
Letters

THE MARRIAGE

(1833–1842)

Or: The Man Who Didn't Want the Woman

"It is the reward of virtue. It is a marriage from the last chapter of one of Mme. Sand's novels," said my mother. "It is the reward of vice. It is a marriage from the end of a Balzac novel," thought I.
— Marcel Proust, *Albertine Disparue*

Some people think Gogol was buried alive. What is certain is that the manner of his dying was so horrible that, in any version, it reads like a fiction of Hoffmann or Poe. This comedian, like others, was not merely melancholic and hypochondriac, as many, including himself, have stressed. He was one of the most tormented of men, a Saint Anthony beset by horrid temptations, a Saint Sebastian riddled with ugly arrows, yet not, of course, a Saint at all. He could create idylls, some of which are convincing, and he could also create infernos, all of which are convincing.

Thoreau maintained that most men lead lives of quiet desperation. Gogol would have agreed with him, save for the quietness. He can *say* "Never mind, never mind, silence!" but actually:

> They dripped cold water on my head ... It was hell. They could hardly hold me down, I was in such a frenzy ... Save your son, Mother, shed a tear on his aching head, they are tormenting him, there is no place for him in the whole wide world, they are hunting him down!

In English literature, the only suffering as bad as this is that of Lear, and Shakespeare can only get away with it as Gogol does: through comedy. For, as well as tragedy, *King Lear* is a comedy of the grotesque. This way the suffering becomes bearable: we permit it entrance into art and into our receiving apparatus, though it thereby becomes—in another sense—even less bearable, brings us a vision of a world even less tolerable, a world actual yet unimaginable, a world we cannot deny the reality of but yet which nothing in our upbringing, our religion, our philosophy, our common sense even, has prepared us for.

I have noticed that students who give *A Madman's Diary* just a quick reading fail to notice that it is fundamentally a record of suffering. It is Gogol's art that makes such a reading, superficial as it is, possible. It is as if he were saying: "Life offers the same possibility. If you avoid looking closely into life, you won't find it such a painful affair, and lucky you!" An actor playing my shortened version of the great monologue should make a similar response possible—on the same terms. Someone wandering into the theatre without fully taking in what is transpiring there should be able to think, should be *made* to think, "Oh, look, a clown! And listen, what he says is quite funny and full of amusing fantasy! Enjoy!"

Without enjoyment, it wouldn't be art, but, with enjoyment, on that plane, it is not yet the art of Gogol, for even the serenity of the piece, which does exist, can only be found on the other side of its sea of troubles. You have to wade through the troubles to reach that farther bank where such things as a wart under the nose of the Bey of Algiers can be observed in tranquillity, or, for that matter, where you can conclude that R. D. Laing was anticipated by Gogol, since they both find sense in nonsense, reason in madness, and conversely much nonsense in sensible people, not much sanity in the sane.

"A mad world, my masters! Only you don't agree, do you?" says Gogol, "you agree, rather, with Poprishchin, who considers that he himself is sane and that his torturers are sane Spaniards just performing 'strange' courtly rituals. I must let you keep that illusion. You may find my monologue funny. It *is* funny. That is no illusion. I *am* a humorist. But if you are prepared to immerse yourself in my text—or a performance thereof—I may hope to give you, here and there, a tremor, make you feel a qualm, cause you to raise your hand to your brow in dizziness. 'Mother! Have pity on your sick little boy!' Did that line turn a knife in your gut? Ever so slightly? 'Never mind, never mind, silence!' 'The Bey of Algiers has a wart right under his nose.' "

INSPECTOR

(1834–1836)

Or: When Mother and Daughter Want the Same Man

> What rapture, Oh, it is to know
> A good thing when you see it
> But having known a good thing, oh,
> What rapture 'tis to flee it!
> — Bertolt Brecht,
> *The Good Woman of Setzuan*

At the end of *Gamblers,* the protagonist hurls a deck of cards at the door and it spills all over the floor. A simple enough incident, it might seem, in no way calling to mind the "humanized" playing cards of *Alice in Wonderland.* Yet we realize today that Gogol has more in common with Lewis Carroll than with the Naturalists of his and Carroll's century or with the Socialist Realists of this one, and, some decades before Carroll, he did "humanize" the cards:

> Look at this deck. I should call it the pearl of great price. No, it's more human than that. I shall call it Adelaide. Adelaide, darling, be faithful to me, won't you? Like your little sister here that won me a cool eighty thousand? Only be faithful, Adelaide, and when we get home, I'll have a monument built in your honor . . .

And so, when the stage direction announces that Adelaide is hurled at the door, and Gogol adds that "queens and deuces fly to the floor," we are willing to hear Simon Karlinsky tell us the following about the Russian words used:

> The word for 'queens' in a card deck is actually 'ladies.' The expression 'fly to the floor' can be interpreted to mean 'collapse.' The phrase is thus the climax of the headlong flight from women, love and marriage which gathered ever greater momentum in each of Gogol's succeeding plays. Khlestakov (in *The Inspector General*) fled from marriage in a troika, Podkolyossin in *The Marriage* escaped it by jumping out the window, while at the end of *Gamblers* the very possibility of associating with 'ladies' (either real ones or those made of cardboard) and forming 'couples' with them falls on the floor and collapses.

This would mean that, if Karlinsky is correct, and I think he is, Gogol's stories and plays have, to say the least, a highly personal slant, embody a personal attitude that is special, not to say neurotic: panic at specifically the thought of union with a woman and in general fear of the female sex.

Can comedy be this idiosyncratic? Must it not, rather, incorporate *everyone's* attitudes? Must it not be in the mainstream of tradition, of the conventional wisdom? Must it not bolster those ideas and institutions which themselves bolster society as we know it? Although I am not willing to cry No! in the face of these somewhat rhetorical questions, I would wish to enter three observations which do not add up to a Yes.

First, while the vision of life in *Gamblers* is rooted in its author's "peculiarities," the root is not the flower, and there are transpositions and transformations in this our life by which the "peculiar" is changed into the typical. While Karlinsky's remarks would seem to imply that the play's center of gravity is in sexuality, I would propose, rather, that it has been shifted to the life of "men without women," men without love, men without sex. Incidentally, they are also men without homosexuality, men without even fraternity. Their utter lack of common charity might bring to mind St. Paul's dictum that without charity we are *nothing*. Reactionary as Gogol's politics might be, he is here at one with Marx in exhibiting a form of "living together" which is all money and manipulation. All. So that, as Jan Kott says, the cheats cheat each other, and about this the audience itself is cheated. I would add that, finally, the spectator realizes that he too is a cheat in a world of cheats. "When I consider life, it's *all* a cheat." All. All.

Second, Gogol's peculiarities are not as peculiar as all that. Homosexuals are not a rarity, nor is it rare for someone who defines himself as heterosexual to feel homosexual impulses. But, of course, outright homosexuality is not the issue, as it is not, could not be, overtly presented in Gogol's work: only some of his "symptoms," and notably his aversion to—turning away from—women. What is a rarity in our culture is the male who can cross his heart and say he has never felt this aversion. The culture *as a whole* is anti-feminine in its bias, in its feelings, which is only another way of saying that what we have got—what we have had for many centuries—is male supremacy, a fact of rule, of domination, which spreads out into a million facts of mores and psychology.

In *Man and Superman* Bernard Shaw flies in the face of literary custom by having the woman chase the man while the man runs away. This is effective theatre because the surprise of the spectator, male or female, is linked with a shock of recognition: "this is not supposed to be true but it is." So with Agafya and Podkolyossin in *The Marriage*. So with Poprishchin's withdrawal from the fantasy of erotic romance into the fantasy of political power in *A Madman's Diary*. So with Iharev's *espousal* (that is the word!) of a deck of cards. The thought of Gogol's "peculiarity" can only carry us back to the adage: "all the world's queer save thee and me, and even thee's a little queer."

but *comedy is a game played for money;* and life is no fun for Mr. Ootesh's victims, or not for long. For the audience, the comedy is the blackest of the black: not for nothing did Gogol arrange to have written on his tombstone these words, attributed to Jeremiah: "Through my bitter word I shall laugh."

Other comic writers before Gogol—Machiavelli, Ben Jonson— have been harsh, harsher indeed than Gogol. What they do not have in common with Gogol—though he has it in common with Wilde— is lightness of tone and texture in works which so utterly, so "unlightly" reject the current way of the world, the "world as it is." It may be said of Oscar Wilde that he made of this contrast the very Idea of his best play, for the play called *The Importance of Being Earnest* is really a play about the unimportance of being earnest and the importance of being un-earnest, flippant, dandiacal, "campy." It is the play about everything that pretends to be the play about nothing; and there is a suitable irony in the fact that critics have generally taken it to be the play about nothing that pretends to be the play about everything. A critic is by definition a square—name of Ernest (earnest).

Is Gogol a very different case from Wilde? Even his admirers often decline to accompany him on his journey to his own comic goal. Vladimir Nabokov writes *The Marriage* down as "rather slipshod," and Vsevolod Setchkarev finds that *Gamblers* never could have turned out right because "the original plan for the work was faulty . . . it is not possible to construct a whole play on the basis of this device . . . genuine characterization is impossible from the outset." "Not possible," "impossible" . . . and why? "Too many improbabilities result, and in the end one feels dissatisfied with all the effort expended on a mere trifle." Which is like blaming Wilde for the effort of trying to get his whole critique of bourgeois culture into a "trifle" like *The Importance of Being Earnest*. Which in turn is like saying Mozart shouldn't have composed *Cosí fan tutte,* since a message of that magnitude required a vehicle like *Parsifal* or *Mourning Becomes Electra*.

As for those "too many improbabilities," what is the right number, and who says so?

If Setchkarev finds *Gamblers* too frivolous, D.S. Mirsky—I am limiting my illustrations to really distinguished scholars—finds it too "unpleasant":

> . . . inferior to the two great comedies. It is an unpleasant play, in-
> habited by scoundrels that are not funny and, though the construction is
> neat, it is dry and lacks the richness of the true Gogol.

Evidently Mirsky is not willing to see that "dryness" can have its own "richness," as in wine, and as in much of 20th century literature—though, to be fair, most of this latter has been written since Mirsky's day (by Beckett, Pinter, and others).

The grumble against *Gamblers* would seem to be that, if it is so serious, it shouldn't be so unserious, and, if it is so unserious, it shouldn't be so serious. Yet that strange, that bizarre contrast of tone with intention, of form, if you like, with content, is Nikolai Gogol, and those who wish him otherwise must look for him in the didactic, unironic vein of many of his letters and all of *Selected Passages from Correspondence with Friends.* Alas!

Even the few who admire the didactic writings could scarcely wish away the other works, for they know that it is by his "absurdity," his "impossibility" that Gogol the artist has lived—for over a century now—in the hearts of readers and spectators all over the world. And those who grant him his premises, declining to rule anything out as "impossible from the outset," will go on to grant that he achieved, finally, what at the outset had to seem impossible: a combination of gravity with mischievousness, exact observation with unbridled fantasy, even of seemingly uncontrolled garrulousness with magisterially controlled rhythm, that is uniquely his.

So, having cited Nabokov's low opinion of *The Marriage,* I should like to cite here his appraisal of Gogol at his best: "the greatest artist that Russia has yet produced," adding that, in my view, Gogol is at his best, not only, as Nabokov proposes, in *A Madman's Diary* and *Inspector*, but also in *The Marriage* and *Gamblers.*

THE MARRIAGE

A Comedy in Three Scenes

Characters:

PODKOLYOSSIN, *a Court Councilor in the Civil Service, a*
    bachelor
STEPAN, *his servant*
MADAM FYOKLA, *a matchmaker*
KOTCHKAREV, *a married friend of Podkolyossin*
MISS AGAFYA, *an unmarried lady of twenty-six*
ARINA, *her aunt*
DUNYASHKA, *maid to Agafya and Arina*
MR. OMELET* , *an Assessor in the Civil Service, a bachelor*
MR. ANUTCHKIN, *a gentleman of refined tastes, also a bachelor*
MR. ZEVAKIN, *naval lieutenant, retired, also a bachelor*

Time:

   Circa 1830

Place:

   St. Petersburg

SCENE ONE

A room: bachelor's quarters. PODKOLYOSSIN *is lying alone on a*
couch, smoking his pipe.

PODKOLYOSSIN. I suppose there's nothing else to be done. When
    you finally manage to think it out, you realize you *have* to get
    married: a man can't go on like this, it's too revolting. But I'm

---

*Simon Karlinsky, in his book on Gogol, points out that this is not the only
one of the names in the cast that has, or hints at, a meaning. Zevakin
(Zhevakin) means Chewer. Anutchkin is derived from a word for a footcloth.
Starikov means Old Folks. Podkolyossin means Under the Wheel. In earlier
drafts, Kotchkarev was called Kogtin: Claws. Karlinsky proposes to call
Omelet "Sunny Side Up."

(Enter STEPAN.)

PODKOLYOSSIN. You bought the shoe polish, Stepan?

STEPAN. Yes, sir.

PODKOLYOSSIN. Where? On Voznessensky Avenue? As I told you?

STEPAN. Yes, sir.

PODKOLYOSSIN. Is it any good?

STEPAN. Yes, sir. It's very good, sir.

PODKOLYOSSIN. Have you tried shining my shoes with it?

STEPAN. Yes, sir.

PODKOLYOSSIN. You got a good shine on them?

STEPAN. Not bad, sir.

PODKOLYOSSIN. I'm glad. *(Pause.)* When he gave you that shoe polish, I suppose he asked why in God's name your master wanted it?

STEPAN. No, sir.

PODKOLYOSSIN. Yes, he did. He said: "Aha! So your master's thinking of marriage!" Didn't he?

STEPAN. No, sir.

PODKOLYOSSIN. Thank you, Stepan. You may leave.

(Exit STEPAN.)

PODKOLYOSSIN. It's all very well to say shoes don't matter but, if our shoes weren't well made and well polished, would we be treated with the same respect in polite society? Of course not. Shoes do matter. Then there's the question of corns, I can stand anything but corns. *(Calling:)* Stepan!

STEPAN. Yes, sir!

PODKOLYOSSIN. Did you tell the shoemaker not to give your master corns, Stepan?

STEPAN. Yes, sir.

PODKOLYOSSIN. And what did he say?

STEPAN. He said: "Anything to oblige."

PODKOLYOSSIN. Thank you, Stepan. You may leave.

(Exit STEPAN.)

PODKOLYOSSIN. Details, formalities, practicalities, responsibilities! Do this, do that, and don't forget the other! Getting married, my dear Podkolyossin, is more easily said than done. *(Calling:)* Stepan!

(Enter STEPAN.)

As I was just about to remark . . .

STEPAN. She's here now, sir.

PODKOLYOSSIN. Madam Fyokla?

STEPAN. Madam Fyokla, sir.

PODKOLYOSSIN. Then what are you waiting for? Show her in.

(Exit STEPAN.)

Getting married, my dear Podkolyossin, might be described as an arduous process.

(Enter MADAM FYOKLA.)

Ah, how are you, Madam Fyokla, how goes it? Sit down and tell me. What's her name? Melanie?

FYOKLA. Agafya, sir.

PODKOLYOSSIN. Agafya. Ah, yes. An old maid, I suppose. Forty, if she's a day.

FYOKLA. The idea! Why, when you're married, you'll love her more every hour. You'll live to thank the good Lord I found you such a jewel.

PODKOLYOSSIN. The only trouble is you're such a liar, Madam Fyokla.

FYOKLA. Oh no, sir. I hate liars, sir. Anyhow, I'm too old for it.

PODKOLYOSSIN. How about the dowry? I never did have that clear. Shall we go over the ground again?

FYOKLA. The dowry! Why, it's a brick house in the Moscow section. A regular gold mine. What tenants! The grocer's rent alone amounts to seven hundred. Then there's a saloon in the cellar that does fine business. Then there's the two annexes, one wooden, one on a brick foundation, each one brings in its four hundred a year in rent. Then, in the Viborg suburb*,

---

*The "Moscow section" and "Viborg suburb"—of St. Petersburg of course.

there's a kitchen garden. A merchant has been growing cabbages in it for three years. Good man, never touches a drop, has three sons, married two of 'em off, says the third is still young. "Let him help out in the store for a while," he says. "Myself, I'm old," he says, "let the boy stay in the store a while and help out, let the boy . . ."

PODKOLYOSSIN. Yes, yes. (Pause.) What's she like?

FYOKLA. Peaches and cream. Pink and white roses. Words fail me, Mr. Podkolyossin. All I can say is, if you don't go down on your knees in joy and gratitude, if you don't live to thank me from the depths of your soul and praise me to the azure skies above, well, my name ain't Madam Fyokla, that's all.

PODKOLYOSSIN. So she's no lady.

FYOKLA. Oh, that, sir. Her father's a merchant, what of it? A General would be proud to have her. You don't think she'd marry a merchant? "No," says she, "let me not be ruled by outward show. What care I if he's not good-looking? It's the man inside that matters. He must be gently born!" Genteel ain't the word, you ought to hear the rustling of her silks of a Sunday! She's a princess.

PODKOLYOSSIN. Now, Madam Fyokla, you realize that I am a Court Councilor and that that's why I asked you . . .

FYOKLA. Course I realize. We've had a Court Councilor already. She refused him. Didn't like him, that was the trouble. Nice-looking gentleman, but special. Every time he opened his mouth, out came a lie. Well, God made us all. The poor fellow can't help it, the lies just come rolling out. God's will be done!

PODKOLYOSSIN. Madam Fyokla, haven't you got any others?

FYOKLA. Others?! What's wrong with her?

PODKOLYOSSIN. She's the best you can do?

FYOKLA. She's the best anyone could do. You could roam the seven seas and never find her like.

PODKOLYOSSIN. I see. Then I must think it over, mustn't I? Come back the day after tomorrow. We'll talk about it. I shall lie on this couch and you can tell your story . . .

FYOKLA. Oh dear, we've been carrying on this way for three months, and where has it got us? You just sit around in your bathrobe and smoke your pipe!

PODKOLYOSSIN. My dear Madam Fyokla, you think getting married is no more than calling for your shoes and taking a walk. No, Madam Fyokla. One must ponder. One must look into it.

FYOKLA. Surely, surely. Go ponder. Go look into it. The goods are certainly there to be looked at. Have that Stepan bring you your coat and drive you to Miss Agafya's while it's still morning.

PODKOLYOSSIN. Now? The weather looks awfully uncertain to me. If I go out, it's sure to rain.

FYOKLA. It's your loss, Mr. Podkolyossin. Your hair's turning gray, how much longer will you be in the running? Being a Court Councilor won't help. We can easily do better than that. We'll never give you a second look.

PODKOLYOSSIN. What? What was that? What do you mean by saying I have gray hair? Where? I never noticed—*(He feels his hair.)*

FYOKLA. Course you have gray hair. How shouldn't you have? So watch yourself with your: "Haven't you got any others?" or I'll turn my attention to a certain Captain of Lancers, head and shoulders taller than you, and a voice like a trombone.

PODKOLYOSSIN. It's not true. Where's that mirror? What on earth gave you the idea I'm gray? Stepan, a mirror! No, no, I'll get it myself. What next? God help us, this is worse than smallpox.

(Exit PODKOLYOSSIN. Enter KOTCHKAREV, running.)

KOTCHKAREV. Where's Podkolyossin? What are you doing here? Oh, it's you. Tell me something: what made you find me a wife?

FYOKLA. Marriages are made in heaven. How are you, Mr. Kotchkarev?

KOTCHKAREV. Heaven? Marriage is hell, my dear woman. In short, I could have done without her.

FYOKLA. Hypocrite! It was what you wanted. "A wife, a wife, my kingdom for a wife!" You've buttered your bread, you must lie on it.

KOTCHKAREV. You hag! But what are you doing here? Surely Podkolyossin isn't thinking of . . .?

FYOKLA. No? God's will be done.

KOTCHKAREV. Well, well, well! The rascal never said a thing to me. He's a sly one.

(Enter PODKOLYOSSIN *carrying a mirror and looking hard into it.)*

KOTCHKAREV *(creeping up behind him).* Boom!

PODKOLYOSSIN *(dropping the mirror with a shriek).* Are you crazy? You've given me heart failure.

KOTCHKAREV. Can't you take a joke? Ha! ha! ha!

PODKOLYOSSIN. Joke? You scared me to death. And I've broken the mirror. Now, really, Kotchkarev, I must scold you. That was a very valuable mirror. Imported from England.

KOTCHKAREV. Oh, come, I can find you another mirror.

PODKOLYOSSIN. I know the sort of mirror *you'll* dig up. Very nice, except that I'll look ten years older in it, and all twisted out of shape.

KOTCHKAREV. Now, don't be unfair, Podkolyossin. I'm the one with reason to grumble. You hide everything from me.

PODKOLYOSSIN. Such as what, my friend?

KOTCHKAREV. Aren't you thinking of marriage?

PODKOLYOSSIN. What? Why, of course not!

KOTCHKAREV. Sorry, but I have proof.

PODKOLYOSSIN. Where?

KOTCHKAREV. There. *(He points to* FYOKLA.*)* The living symbol of matrimony. Mind you, I'm not objecting. What's wrong with matrimony? Isn't it a Christian duty? A service to Holy Russia? Good. Let me take things in hand. *(To* FYOKLA.*)* You! Tell me who's who, why's why, and how's how. What's her father—nobleman, merchant, civil servant? What's her name?

FYOKLA. Agafya.

KOTCHKAREV. Agafya Brandalistov?

FYOKLA. No. Agafya Kooperdyagin.

KOTCHKAREV. I know her well! She lives in Shop Street.

FYOKLA. No. This one lives in Soap Street.

KOTCHKAREV. That's right. Soap Street. The wooden house just the other side the store.

FYOKLA. No. The brick house this side the tavern.

KOTCHKAREV. The tavern?

FYOKLA. You turn into Soap Street, you pass the sentry box, and the house is straight in front of you. I mean, the house straight in front of you is the one where that dressmaker lives, the one that was the Senator's mistress. Don't go in. There's another house right next door, a brick house, and that's the one where Miss Agafya lives.

KOTCHKAREV. Very well, my good woman. Now, just leave everything to me, and clear out. You're not needed.

FYOKLA. What? You think you can arrange the marriage yourself?

KOTCHKAREV. Exactly. And I'm advising you not to meddle. I'm advising you.

FYOKLA. You son of a—Incidentally, this is no business for the son of anything. It's a woman's job!

KOTCHKAREV. Now run along, my dear madam. You are out of your depth. Leave us!

FYOKLA. The idea! Taking the bread right out of my mouth! Meddler! Atheist! If only I'd known, my lips would have been sealed.

(Exit FYOKLA *in high dudgeon.)*

KOTCHKAREV. Podkolyossin, there's not a moment to lose. Let's go!

PODKOLYOSSIN. But, my dear Kotchkarev, I'm not at all certain . . .

KOTCHKAREV. Stuff! Nonsense! You mustn't be shy, that's all.

PODKOLYOSSIN. Mustn't be . . .?

KOTCHKAREV. Well, *be* shy then. I'll get you married so you won't even notice.

PODKOLYOSSIN. But how can you . . .?

KOTCHKAREV. It's easy. We'll go straight to the young lady.

PODKOLYOSSIN. Now?

KOTCHKAREV. Now. You'll be surprised how quickly such a matter can be cleaned up.

PODKOLYOSSIN. Oh dear. I think tomorrow would . . .

KOTCHKAREV. Never put off till tomorrow what you can do today.

PODKOLYOSSIN. Very well. Let's be going.

KOTCHKAREV. Stepan! Bring your master's things! Quick!

(Enter STEPAN.)

PODKOLYOSSIN *(dressing at the mirror).* I must keep you waiting just one minute, old man. I'm putting on my white waistcoat. The occasion requires it.

KOTCHKAREV. No, no, no, go just as you are.

PODKOLYOSSIN *(struggling with his collar).* My collar won't stand up properly, there's no starch in it. Stepan, tell the laundress I'll give her one more chance, after which my patience will be at an end. There's a man in the picture, I'll be bound. Instead of starching my collars, she's carrying on with a man. I don't know what the working class is coming to.

KOTCHKAREV. The working class can wait. Let's you and I get going, Podkolyossin.

PODKOLYOSSIN. One more second. My coat. *(He puts on his coat. He is ready. Suddenly he sits down.)* I have a suggestion, Kotchkarev. You go. Go by yourself.

KOTCHKAREV. Go by myself, are you crazy? Which of us is getting married, you or me?

PODKOLYOSSIN. You have a point. There's no denying that. But I don't feel like it.

KOTCHKAREV. You don't . . .?

PODKOLYOSSIN. How about tomorrow?

KOTCHKAREV. Tomorrow! You fool! You prize idiot! Here you are, dressed and ready, and all of a sudden, you "don't feel like it." Podkolyossin, I hate to say it, but you're rather a pig.

PODKOLYOSSIN. Possibly. But what have I done to you, Kotchkarev? Couldn't you just leave me alone?

KOTCHKAREV. My thesis is that you're a fool, I believe there's even a consensus of opinion on the subject. You're an idiot, quite simply an idiot, though incidentally and into the bargain a Court Councilor.

PODKOLYOSSIN. They why in God's name . . .?

KOTCHKAREV. . . . waste my time on you? I have a sense of your interests, even if you don't. Podkolyossin, someone else will get her if you don't watch out.

PODKOLYOSSIN. But why . . .?

KOTCHKAREV. I can't stand bachelors. It wouldn't bother me if there weren't a single bachelor left in the world. Oh, if only you could see yourself, you're a nincompoop, you're a . . . I just thought of a wonderful word for you but it wouldn't pass the censor. You're an old woman. Leave it at that.

PODKOLYOSSIN. I say, that's going rather far, you know. *(Aside* to KOTCHKAREV:) Don't you realize my servant is in the room? Please moderate your language!

KOTCHKAREV. No one respects moderation more than I, but you've made it impossible for me—*(Roaring:)*—by being such an idiot! *(More quietly:)* I can't help shouting at you. No one could help shouting at you. Here you were with your mind made up, an honest, decent candidate for marriage, listening quietly to the voice of reason and then, presto, you go plumb crazy right in front of my eyes. *(Shouting:)* You fool! You idiot! You old woman! *(Quietly:)* Are you coming?

PODKOLYOSSIN. Of course, I'm coming, my dear Kotchkarev. What's all the fuss about?

KOTCHKAREV. Ah! You're coming? Stepan! Your master's hat and coat!

PODKOLYOSSIN. Really, Kotchkarev, you're rather a card. All this name-calling for no reason at all. I'm afraid you have no manners, my dear Kotchkarev.

KOTCHKAREV. But you *are* coming?

PODKOLYOSSIN. Why, of course, my dear Kotchkarev.

(Exeunt.)

SCENE TWO

A room in AGAFYA'S *brick house in the Moscow section.*

AGAFYA *is dealing cards for fortune telling. Her aunt* ARINA *looks over her shoulder.*

AGAFYA. Another journey, Aunt Arina! A king of diamonds is interested . . . tears . . . a love letter! Here on the left a king of clubs shows himself capable of real feeling, but a wicked woman is an obstacle in his path.

ARINA. Now who's the king of clubs? Who would you say he is, my dear Agafya?

AGAFYA. I really don't know, Aunt.

ARINA. I do, my dear.

AGAFYA. Really? Who?

ARINA. A certain merchant. In the cloth business. Doing very nicely. His name is Starikov.

AGAFYA. Oh, no, no, no. Not him. I could swear it's not him.

ARINA. Of course it is. Starikov has black hair. Obviously the king of clubs, my dear.

AGAFYA. Nothing of the kind, Aunt. A merchant couldn't be a king. It must be some fine gentleman!

ARINA. Oh dear, Agafya, what would your sainted father say if he could hear you? I can see him now, banging the table and shouting: "I'll give my daughter to no whippersnapper of a Colonel! Is anyone here ashamed to be a merchant? I'll spit in his eye." Father Kooperdyagin, where are you now? "Others may do as they choose," he'd say, and the table would shake under his big fist, "others may do as they choose, but no son of mine's going into the Civil Service! What this country needs is good merchants!" He had big hands, and a bigger temper! I'm sure he was the death of your poor mother. But for him, she might be living still.

AGAFYA. You see! A girl just shouldn't marry a merchant. They don't know how to behave.

ARINA. Starikov is different, my dear.

AGAFYA. I won't have him, that's all! As soon as he starts eating, everything dribbles down his beard. Ugh!

ARINA. How can you possibly do any better, my dear?

AGAFYA. With the help of Madam Fyokla, dear Aunt. She has promised to find me a husband of the very highest quality.

ARINA. But then she's a notorious liar, my dear.

(Enter FYOKLA.)

FYOKLA. I work my hands to the bone for you, and what is my reward? Slander!

AGAFYA. Madam Fyokla! Oh! What news? Have you found one?

FYOKLA. One? I've found you half a dozen. All of the highest quality. But first let me catch my breath, I'm done up, I've been working like a demon: houses, offices, army barracks, government departments. And I nearly got a beating for my pains—from that horrible old woman that married the Aferovs—she screamed at me. "You're taking the bread right out of my mouth!" says she. "You stick to your district," says she, "this is my territory." "That's all very well," says I, "but for Miss Agafya I'll go through fire, I'll even go through your district, so keep your hair on." And what husbands I've picked for you! Greatest bunch of bridegrooms in the history of the world. And they'll start coming today. I ran ahead to warn you.

AGAFYA. Today! Ooh! I'm scared!

FYOKLA. Take it easy, my dear, it's just the usual. *They* take a look at you, *you* take a look at them. If mutual satisfaction does not result, you go your several ways, that's life.

ARINA. A nice batch of bums you've knocked together, I'll be sworn.

AGAFYA. How many did you say, Madam Fyokla?

FYOKLA. Six. Six specimens of the masculine gender at its brightest and best.

AGAFYA. Six! Ooh!

FYOKLA. Nothing to be in a state about, my dear. It's always best to have a choice—in any line of merchandise.

AGAFYA. They're all fine gentlemen, I hope?

FYOKLA. Every man jack. I never saw such gentlemanly gentlemen in all my life.

AGAFYA. What are they like? Tell me about them.

FYOKLA. Special reserve stock. Grade A. You don't see such high-quality stuff any more. Mr. Zevakin, for instance. What a gentleman! He even served in the Navy. I guess you should take him. He told me himself he had to have "a girl with some flesh on her bones, never could stand a skeleton in skirts, no, ma'am." Course, if you want a *very* grand gentleman, you should take Ivan Pavlovitch. A big shot in the Civil Service. An Assessor. Big as a barrel and twice as human! "With me you can cut the cackle," he roars, "cut the cackle and tell me straight: what has she got in real estate and what has she got in cash?" I gave him a rough idea. "You're lying, daughter of a dog!" he roared, "you're lying, you . . ." Then he used a dirty word I musn't repeat. I could tell he was a very important person.

AGAFYA. Who else? Who else is there?

FYOKLA. There's Mr. Anutchkin. A model of refinement with delicious lips—like raspberries. Nice too. "I want a wife," says he, "that's both pretty and educated. I want a wife," says he, "that speaks French." A man of culture. Very delicate, very refined. His legs are as slender as a girl's arms.

AGAFYA. Slender! But a slender man isn't . . . I don't like slender men.

FYOKLA. Then take Ivan Pavlovitch. He's a gentleman, if anyone is. He's such a tremendous gentleman he can hardly get through the doorway.

AGAFYA. How old is he, Madam Fyokla?

FYOKLA. Not old at all, he's young, not much more than fifty, maybe less.

AGAFYA. What's his last name?

FYOKLA. Omelet.

AGAFYA. I beg your pardon.

FYOKLA. That's his name. Ivan Pavlovitch Omelet.

AGAFYA. No.

FYOKLA. Yes.

AGAFYA. Mrs. Agafya Omelet. Ugh!

FYOKLA. Russian names are queer. When you hear them, you can only spit and cross yourself.

AGAFYA. Mrs. Agafya Omelet. No!

FYOKLA. Then take Mr. Zevakin, he's nice too.

AGAFYA. How's his hair?

FYOKLA. Nice.

AGAFYA. And his nose?

FYOKLA. Handsome. All of him's handsome, nothing wrong, nothing missing, everything just exactly in place, he's a very tidy man. Course, we all have our ways, and he . . . has it in for furniture.

AGAFYA. Has it in for furniture?

FYOKLA. Something like that. 'T any rate, he don't have any. Not a stick. His apartment is naked as a newborn babe. Nothing but a stovepipe.

AGAFYA. Who else is there, Madam Fyokla?

FYOKLA. Mr. Pantylayoff, another civil servant. Stammers a little bit, but he's very well behaved.

ARINA. You and your civil servants! I'll bet he drinks like a fish. Doesn't he?

FYOKLA. He does take a drink once in a while. That can't be helped, he's real high up in the service. And soft as silk.

AGAFYA. No, no, I wouldn't fancy marrying a drunk.

FYOKLA. As you say, my dear. If you don't like one, take another. Though, after all, taking a drink once in a while, it's not like he was drunk every day in the week. Some days he's dead sober.

AGAFYA. Who else is there, Madam Fyokla?

FYOKLA. Right now I've only one left, Miss Agafya, and I have to admit he's rather . . . But God made him! Take one of the others.

AGAFYA. But who is this one?

FYOKLA. I wasn't going to mention him, if you must know. Yes, he's a Court Councilor, he wears the ribbon in his buttonhole, that's when he wears a buttonhole: in general, he's home in his robe, there's's no getting him out of the house.

AGAFYA. Then who else is there? That only makes five. You said there were six.

FYOKLA. Five's enough, ain't it? Don't be so greedy. A minute ago five was too many for you.

ARINA. What good are these fine gentlemen, five or six? One merchant would be worth the lot.

FYOKLA. Oh no, ma'am. Gentlemen are much more highly thought of than merchants!

ARINA. Give me the merchant Starikov. Can't you just see him in his black cap driving his sleigh on winter roads . . .

then be stuck, when you're married, with nothing but feather beds and pillows!

(The bell rings. DUNYASHKA *runs across the room on her way to the door. Voices. Enter* ANUTCHKIN *and* DUNYASHKA.)

DUNYASHKA. Will you wait here, sir?

(Exit DUNYASHKA.)

(OMELET *and* ANUTCHKIN *bow to each other.)*

OMELET. Good day to you, sir.

ANUTCHKIN. Oh, good day, sir. Oh! I haven't the honor of addressing the dear young lady's dear papa?

OMELET. No, sir, you haven't. I am nobody's papa, sir. I am a bachelor.

ANUTCHKIN *(with a little cry).* Oh! I've put my foot in it. Oh! I beg your pardon, sir!

OMELET *(aside).* I wouldn't trust this fellow an inch. That hangdog look of his strongly suggests he may have come on the same errand as myself. *(To* ANUTCHKIN:) You have business with the lady of the house, sir?

ANUTCHKIN. Business? Um, no, sir. I just happened to be passing, so I thought I'd, um, drop in, sir.

OMELET *(aside).* He can hardly expect me to believe that. Obviously, he wants to get himself married, the crook.

(The bell rings. DUNYASHKA *crosses as before. Voices.)*

(Enter DUNYASHKA *and* ZEVAKIN.)

ZEVAKIN. Brush me off, would you, my dear? You can't imagine how dusty it is outside. Get that bit of fluff off, would you, my dear? Yes, that speck there. *(He turns around.)* Isn't that a spider on my coattail? No? Thank you, my dear. Now the sleeves! *(He strokes his sleeve with his hand, while glancing at* ANUTCHKIN *and* OMELET.) English cloth, don't you know. Wears forever. Bought it in '95 when the squadron was in Sicily. Was a midshipman at the time, had my uniform made of it. Was promoted to lieutenant—1801 it must have been—it still looked new. Sailed round the world in 1814—it wasn't more than a little frayed at the seams. One year later, left the Navy, had it turned. Been wearing it that way ten years, it's still like new. Thank you, my dear. You're pretty, did anyone ever tell you? (*He kisses his hand to her, goes to the mirror, slightly ruffles his hair.*)

ANUTCHKIN. Sicily did you say, sir? How interesting! May I ask what it's like?

ZEVAKIN. Spent thirty-four days there. The view is ravishing. What mountains! What pomegranate trees! And what girls! Girls—everywhere you look!

ANUTCHKIN. They're not very well educated, are they?

ZEVAKIN. They're superbly educated. Not like Russian girls. More like Russian countesses. Superbly educated! I'd walk down the street in my lieutenant's uniform—epaulets, gold braid, and so forth—and, well, you know how it is—every house with a balcony or a roof you can sit out on, flat as this floor—you look up, don't you know, and on every balcony, on every roof—there's a rose! A gorgeous Sicilian rose!

ANUTCHKIN. They're rather good at horticulture, aren't they?

ZEVAKIN. Terrific! You look up at . . . one rose or another . . . you greet her—(*He bows and waves.*)—as she sits demurely fanning herself—so. (*He indicates that the "rose" gives him a sign.*)

ANUTCHKIN. Oh, you mean young ladies, ha! ha! ha!

Gravely.

They dress with taste?

ZEVAKIN. With impeccable taste. I can see them now: some sort of fluffy silky business in front, earrings all over the place . . . Dainty morsels, by Jove!

ANUTCHKIN. Interesting from so many points of view. Languages, for instance. By the way, what is their language?

ZEVAKIN. French. Of course.

ANUTCHKIN. All your young ladies spoke French?

ZEVAKIN. Every one of them. I was there thirty-four days. Not one word of Russian did they utter.

ANUTCHKIN. Nothing but French?

ZEVAKIN. Not one word of Russian. And I'm not just speaking of gentlemen. No. Take any simple Sicilian peasant with a load of rubbish on his back and say to him in plain Russian: "Give me some bread." And, by Jove, you'll have to translate it into

French for him. *"Dateci del vino!"* you have to say. And he'll reply in perfect French: *"Si signore, subito!"*

OMELET. Life in foreign parts is not without importance, of course. I am glad to make your acquaintance, sir. With whom have I the honor?

ZEVAKIN. Zevakin, at your service. Naval lieutenant, retired. And with whom have *I . . .*?

OMELET. I am a civil servant, sir. Omelet!

ZEVAKIN. Thanks, no. I just ate a pickled herring.

OMELET. You misunderstand me, sir. Omelet is my name.

ZEVAKIN. No! A thousand pardons! I'm rather deaf, don't you know. How silly of me!

OMELET. Russian names! *(He shakes his head.)*

ZEVAKIN. Ah yes, Russian names! In our squadron we had both a Tipsykov and a Topsykov. Then there was a midshipman called Tatters. "Where's rags and tatters?" the captain used to shout. "Where is that rags and tatters?"

(The bell rings. FYOKLA *crosses the room.)*

OMELET. Good day to you, ma'am.

ZEVAKIN. How are you, my dear?

ANUTCHKIN. Good morning, Madam Fyokla.

FYOKLA *(running).* Morning, morning, morning.

(She opens the door. Voices. FYOKLA *is heard to say:)*

("Try to be a man!")

(Enter FYOKLA *with* KOTCHKAREV *and* PODKOLYOSSIN.)*

KOTCHKAREV *(aside to* PODKOLYOSSIN). She's right: try to be a man! *(He looks around and bows in some astonishment. Aside:)* Good God, what a mob! Are they *all* after her? *(Aside to* FYOKLA, *nudging her:)* How'd you pick up all these queer birds?

FYOKLA *(aside to him).* "A gentlemen knows a gentleman when he sees one."

KOTCHKAREV *(aside to her).* "But a guest on the make needs no invitation."

FYOKLA *(aside to him)*. "People in glass houses shouldn't throw stones. Not every man with a feather in his cap has money in his purse."

KOTCHKAREV. "But many a large pocket has a hole in it." *(Aloud.)* Where's the young lady? Ah! The door to her bedroom! *(He goes to the door.)*

FYOKLA. Now stop that! She hasn't finished dressing!

KOTCHKAREV. Aha! She hasn't finished dressing? I will verify that statement. *(He looks through the keyhole.)*

ZEVAKIN. May I too make so bold?

OMELET. Not a bad idea! Let me . . .

ANUTCHKIN. It's not very well bred but . . .

KOTCHKAREV *(at the keyhole)*. Something white, I'm afraid I can't make out if it's a woman or a pillow. *(But they all rush to look.)* Look out, someone's coming!

(They all leave the door hastily. Enter ARINA and AGAFYA. All bow.)

ARINA. And to what do we owe the pleasure, dear sir?

OMELET. Well, ma'am, as a matter of fact, I read in the paper that you wish to sign a contract for the sale of timber. Being a civil servant in the department concerned, I have come to inquire about the, um, particulars.

ARINA. There must be some mistake, sir. But we are glad to see you all the same. Your name, sir?

OMELET. Ivan Pavlovitch Omelet.

ARINA. Omelet?

OMELET. Omelet.

ARINA. Pray be seated, Mr. Omelet. *(Turning to ZEVAKIN.)* And you, sir?

ZEVAKIN. I saw something in the paper too, dear madam. Dashed if I remember what it was. But I thought I'd come, it was a lovely day, the grass was green . . .

ARINA. Your name, sir?

ZEVAKIN. Baltazar Zevakin. Naval lieutenant, retired. To be frank, there was another Zevakin in the Navy, ma'am, no relation. Wounded just below the knee. Bullet hit him in a sinew, went right through, threaded it like a needle, ma'am. Strange chap. Never could stand next to him with any tranquility. Always felt he was going to kick me—with his knee, don't you know.

ARINA. Pray be seated, Mr. Zevakin. *(Turning to* ANUTCHKIN.) And you, dear sir? What brought you along?

ANUTCHKIN. Simple neighborliness, good madam. I'm a neighbor . . .

ARINA. Oh, you're living in Tulobov's house opposite?

ANUTCHKIN. No, ma'am. Not exactly, ma'am.

ARINA. Then you must be living at . . .

ANUTCHKIN. No, ma'am, I'm living in Peski, ma'am. But I'm a neighbor of yours—in the spirit, ha! ha!

ARINA. Your name, sir?

ANUTCHKIN. Anutchkin, ma'am.

ARINA. Pray be seated, Mr. Anutchkin.

Turning to KOTCHKAREV.

And you, dear sir?

KOTCHKAREV. But of course you already know me, ma'am. As I believe you do too, Miss Agafya.

AGAFYA. I don't think I recall . . .

KOTCHKAREV. Reach back in the deeper recesses of your memory. Actually you *must* have met me.

AGAFYA. Really? Could it have been at the Beeryooshkins'?

KOTCHKAREV. Of course it could have been at the Beeryooshkins'.

AGAFYA. Did you hear? Something terrible has happened to Mrs. Beeryooshkin.

KOTCHKAREV. I know. She got married.

AGAFYA. No, no, she broke her leg, sir.

ARINA. A complex fracture. She was coming home late and the coachman was drunk, he upset her in the roadway.

KOTCHKAREV. I couldn't remember whether she got married or only broke her leg, ma'am.

ARINA. And what may your name be, dear sir?

KOTCHKAREV. Ilya Kotchkarev, at your service, ma'am. I'm a relative of yours. I've heard a lot about you from my wife. What's more,

Brings PODKOLYOSSIN *forward.*

I want you to meet my friend Court Councilor Podkolyossin—a name that is known wherever the words "Civil Service" are spoken.

ARINA. What was the name?

KOTCHKAREV. Podkolyossin.

ARINA. He's the head of his department, you say?

KOTCHKAREV. Well, there's a nominal head, of course. But it's Podkolyossin that does the work.*

ARINA. I see. Pray be seated, sirs.

All are seated. Silence.

OMELET. Strange weather we're having. This morning it looked like rain, and now it, um, doesn't look like rain.

AGAFYA. Yes, yes! Isn't it awful? Sometimes raining, sometimes not raining! I hate that.

ZEVAKIN. It reminds me of Sicily. We were there with the squadron, ma'am. February I think it was, they call it spring over there. The sun would shine, and you'd go out. Then it would look like rain, and you'd look up at the sky. Then it would rain, and you had to go back indoors.

OMELET. It's all right as long as you don't have to sit alone in such weather. If you're married, it's quite different, of course. But for a solitary man, it is absolutely . . .

ZEVAKIN. Appalling.

ANUTCHKIN. Oh, I agree.

KOTCHKAREV. So do I! Absolute torture! You wish you were dead. God keep us all from such a fate! *(Pause.)*

---

*Simon Karlinsky has called attention to an earlier draft of the play in which Kotchkarev adds: "At this point he still has a special desk job, but within three days he's sure to head a section of his own. The director of this section, his superior, loves him so much he even sleeps in the same bed with him."

ZEVAKIN. I'll go smoke my pipe. Are you going my way, sir? Where is it you live, sir?

ANUTCHKIN. Live? Oh, yes. In Peski. Petrovsky Lane.

ZEVAKIN. Not exactly on my way, don't you know. But, by God, I'll come with you, sir!

(Exit with ANUTCHKIN.)

PODKOLYOSSIN. I say, Kotchkarev, what are we waiting for?

KOTCHKAREV. Don't you think she's rather sweet?

PODKOLYOSSIN. No. No, I don't. I think she's rather sour.

KOTCHKAREV. Oh, come. You said yourself she was very pretty.

PODKOLYOSSIN. No, no, no. Her nose is too big. And she doesn't know French.

KOTCHKAREV. Good God, man, what do you want her to know French for?

PODKOLYOSSIN. She's a woman, old man.

KOTCHKAREV. What?

PODKOLYOSSIN. A woman who doesn't know French is not a woman.

KOTCHKAREV. My dear Podkolyossin, think for yourself. Before those fools started gabbing, you thought she was quite a beauty.

PODKOLYOSSIN. Perhaps. Yes, she did take my fancy at first. But when they pointed out that her nose was too big, I had to hand it to them: her nose *is* too big.

KOTCHKAREV. Don't you realize they said that just to put you off? I was doing the same to them, telling them I didn't know what they saw in her, and so on. That's *savoir vivre.* The truth, my dear Podkolyossin, is different. Her eyes! They breathe. They speak. What eyes! And her nose! Yes, even her nose! Smooth as monumental alabaster. Smoother. Take another look.

PODKOLYOSSIN. I suppose you're right. She *is* rather pretty.

KOTCHKAREV. Exactly. I have an idea. Now that they've all left, let's you and I go to her, talk the whole thing over, and close the deal.

PODKOLYOSSIN. What? Oh, I couldn't do that.

KOTCHKAREV. Why on earth not?

PODKOLYOSSIN. Oh, I couldn't be so brazen. She has a great many suitors. Let her at least do her own choosing, old man.

KOTCHKAREV. Many suitors? That riffraff! What are you afraid of? I'll take care of them.

PODKOLYOSSIN. You will? How?

KOTCHKAREV. That's my business. All I need from you is a promise not to cry off later.

PODKOLYOSSIN. I won't cry off later. Why should I? Dash it all, I *want* to get married!

KOTCHKAREV. You do?

PODKOLYOSSIN. Oh, I do, I do!

KOTCHKAREV. You'll give me your hand on it?

PODKOLYOSSIN. Why, certainly, old man, of course.

KOTCHKAREV. Shake! *(They shake hands.)* Let's be going then.

PODKOLYOSSIN. Yes, really! I *want* to get married!

(As they leave, the curtain falls.)

SCENE THREE

The setting is the same as Scene Two. AGAFYA *is alone in the room.*

AGAFYA. I'm in quite a quandary. If only there were but one gentleman—or two—or at most three . . . There are four. Mr. Anutchkin isn't bad-looking, though he *is* thin. Mr. Podkolyossin isn't bad-looking either. Then, too, Mr. Omelet is a very prepossessing person, though fat. What am I to do? Mr. Zevakin is a man of parts. I'm in quite a quandary. If one could combine Mr. Anutchkin's lips with Mr. Podkolyossin's nose or Mr. Zevakin's assurance with Mr. Omelet's solidity, a girl might know how to choose! The way things are, it makes my head swim. I know what I'll do: draw lots and trust in God. Find a husband by drawing lots! Write each name on a scrap of paper, screw each bit of paper into a ball, shake the balls up together, and then—God's will be done! *(She goes to a table, cuts up a sheet of paper with scissors, rolls each piece into a ball after writing on it, while continuing to talk.)* A young girl's life is not a happy one, especially not when she's in love. Men don't understand how she feels, men don't even make much of an effort ... Now I'm ready. I drop these in my purse, and shut my eyes while God's will is done on earth as it is in heaven. *(She drops the paper balls in her purse and shakes it.)* Ugh, how scary! I do hope it's Mr. Anutchkin. No, I don't, why did I say that? I'm hoping it's Mr. Podkolyossin. Am I? Why? Why him? What's wrong with the others? Ooh! *(She is breathless with excitement.)* I mustn't. I must pick one, and accept the judgment of God! *(She sticks her hand in the purse. It emerges with all the lots in it.)* All of them, He's giving me all four of them! No, no, what nonsense! My heart's beating like a drum. What is it we believe in, in Russia? Monogamy. One husband to one wife. I must limit myself to one.

(Enter KOTCHKAREV, stealthily. He stands over her shoulder.)

Ooh, I hope it's Mr. Zevakin! No, what am I saying? Mr. Anutchkin's the one I want, which is *his* lot? *(Shocked at herself.)* No! I'll be a good girl: let fate decide.

KOTCHKAREV *(quietly)*. Take Podkolyossin.

(AGAFYA screams, hiding her face in her hands, too scared to look who spoke.)

KOTCHKAREV. He's by far the best of the bunch, what are you so scared of? It's me: Kotchkarev. I said: take Podkolyossin.

AGAFYA. You heard what I was saying!

KOTCHKAREV. What of it, my dear? I'm one of the family, don't mind me. Aren't you letting us see that pretty physiognomy today?

AGAFYA *(half covering her face)*. I'm so ashamed!

KOTCHKAREV. Take Podkolyossin.

(AGAFYA again screams and hides her face in her hands.)

KOTCHKAREV. He's terrific. He's worked miracles in that office of his. Miracles!

AGAFYA *(peeping through her fingers)*. How about the others? Mr. Anutchkin. He's rather nice too.

KOTCHKAREV. Not compared with Podkolyossin.

AGAFYA. Oh?

KOTCHKAREV. No. Podkolyossin is a man of . . . well . . . Nature might stand up and say to a considerable part of the world: this is a man.

AGAFYA. Then there's Mr. Omelet. He's a fine man.

KOTCHKAREV. Not compared with Podkolyossin.

AGAFYA. And there's . . .

KOTCHKAREV. They don't compare with Podkolyossin. Any of 'em.

AGAFYA. Why not, Mr. Kotchkarev?

KOTCHKAREV. Why not? Why not? Well, who are they? A Mr. Omelet? A Mr. Anutchkin? A Mr. Zevakin?

AGAFYA. Well, who is he, Mr. Kotchkarev?

KOTCHKAREV. That's just it: he's Podkolyossin. Podkolyossin! It makes a difference, eh?

AGAFYA. They have nice manners, though, Mr. Kotchkarev, they're well behaved.

KOTCHKAREV. Well behaved? You should see them in their natural habitat. Roughnecks! Hoodlums! I'm sorry, Miss Agafya. I shouldn't have said that. Maybe you'd *like* to be beaten on your wedding night?

AGAFYA. Ooh! Beaten? What a dreadful idea!

KOTCHKAREV. They *are* rather dreadful, as a matter of fact.

AGAFYA. So you advise Mr. Podkolyossin?

KOTCHKAREV. Naturally. *(Aside.)* Now we're getting somewhere. Podkolyossin is waiting in the cake shop opposite. I'll go for him.

AGAFYA. You're sure you advise Podkolyossin?

KOTCHKAREV. Podkolyossin forever!

AGAFYA. How about the others?

KOTCHKAREV. How about them?

AGAFYA. Must I turn them down? All of them?

KOTCHKAREV. I'm afraid so. Polygamy is illegal.

AGAFYA. But how can I, Mr. Kotchkarev? I feel so ashamed!

KOTCHKAREV. Of what? Tell 'em you're not old enough for marriage.

AGAFYA. They might not believe me, Mr. Kotchkarev. They might ask questions.

KOTCHKAREV. In that case, you'll have to take action. Say something drastic.

AGAFYA. Such as what, Mr. Kotchkarev?

KOTCHKAREV. Such as: "Get out of my house, you fools!"

AGAFYA *(with a squeal)*. Oh, I couldn't say a thing like that, Mr. Kotchkarev!

KOTCHKAREV. I think you could. If you tried very, very hard.

AGAFYA. But it's so rude, Mr. Kotchkarev!

KOTCHKAREV. True. But you'll never see them again, so what does it matter?

AGAFYA. It just isn't nice. And they'll be furious!

KOTCHKAREV. What of it? There's nothing they can do. At worst, they can only spit in your face.

AGAFYA. Spit in my . . .?

KOTCHKAREV. Face. It happens. Some of my best friends have been spat on. I recall one in particular, handsome young fellow, he kept pestering his boss for a raise, naturally the boss didn't like it, but the young fellow didn't leave off, so the old boy reached breaking point and spat in his face. "There's your extra pay for this week," he cried, "now get out, you little devil!" Nevertheless, when payday came, the young man found his salary had been raised. The game was worth the candle. Salary in exchange for saliva! Many great expectations realized—at the cost of one expectoration! Russia is a wonderful country. It'd be different if we had no handkerchiefs. But lo! in your pocket, a charming little hanky, a very present help in time of trouble. *(The bell rings.)* That'll be one of your gentlemen. I'll deprive myself of the pleasure. Is there another way out?

AGAFYA. Yes, Mr. Kotchkarev: the back stairs. Oh, I'm all of a tremble!

KOTCHKAREV. Don't worry. Be calm. All will be well. Au revoir! *(Aside.)* And I'll get Podkolyossin and bring him here in short order.

(Exit KOTCHKAREV. Enter OMELET.)

OMELET. Good day, Miss Agafya.

AGAFYA. Oh, good day, Mr. Omelet. May I ask . . .?

OMELET. I'm afraid I'm a little on the early side. Permit me to explain. I must speak with you—alone. Ahem. As for my position in the Civil Service, ma'am, I imagine it is already known to you. I am an Assessor, madam. I assess. All day long I am busy assessing. It is not an unhappy life. Favored by my superiors, obeyed by my subordinates, I lack but one thing, dear lady—or rather one person—a friend, a comrade, a partner along life's way. *(Pause.)* You take my meaning? Cut the cackle and tell me straight. Is it yes?

AGAFYA. Oh, sir, I don't think I'm old enough! *(As* OMELET *starts to protest:)* I mean I'm not thinking of marriage just now.

OMELET. Not thinking of marriage? With a matchmaker running in and out? *(Pulling himself together.)* Pardon me, ma'am, I'm sure I didn't rightly take your meaning. *(The bell rings.)* Damn it all! A man's just getting down to business, when . . .

(Enter ZEVAKIN.)

ZEVAKIN. Afraid I'm a little on the early side, don't you know. *(Seeing* OMELET.) Why, if it isn't Mr. Omelet! How are you, Mr. Omelet?

OMELET *(aside).* When I see you, sir, I feel sick. *(Aloud.)* So what's it to be, madam? Yes or no? *(The bell rings.)* God Almighty!

(Enter ANUTCHKIN.)

ANUTCHKIN. Perhaps, Miss Agafya, I am a little more on the early side than is usual in polite society but . . . *(He sees the others and is overcome.)* Oh!

OMELET *(aside).* Polite society indeed! He has the manners of a billy goat, butting in everywhere. I could break his slender legs. *(Aloud.)* As I was saying, ma'am, what's it to be? I am a busy man. I am extremely short of time. Yes or no?

AGAFYA *(aside).* I don't know what I'm saying. *(Aloud.)* Sir, I really don't think . . . I mean, I really do think . . . Sir, why don't you go?

OMELET. *Go?*

AGAFYA *(aside).* Lord, what have I said?

OMELET. You said go? To me? Go? I'm not acquainted with the word. I'd have to look it up in the Royal Russian Dictionary or

ANUTCHKIN. Not a word?

KOTCHKAREV. Not a syllable. My wife and Miss Agafya went to school together. Brilliant linguist, my wife, I must introduce you to her. Do you know Chinese?

ANUTCHKIN. No, sir.

KOTCHKAREV. I'll have my wife talk Chinese to you. Miss Agafya spent her school days standing in the corner with the dunce's cap on. But the French teacher said that wasn't enough, she should also be flogged.

ANUTCHKIN. I was right. The first moment I set eyes on her I said to myself: "That woman doesn't know a word of French."

OMELET. Oh, damn French! What I want to know is how that out-rageous matchmaker . . . She must be a witch! The lies she told! The house, the annex with the brick foundation, the silver spoons, the sleigh. "Hop in and go for a spin any time the fancy takes you!" says she. That woman can tell a story like one of our Russian novelists. Very good. Just wait till I get my hands on her!

(Enter FYOKLA. OMELET, ANUTCHKIN and KOTCHKAREV all speak at once.)

OMELET. Ah! There she is! Come here, you hag!

ANUTCHKIN. Madam Fyokla, you have deceived me!

KOTCHKAREV. Retribution has overtaken you, Madam Fyokla!

FYOKLA. If you wouldn't all speak at once, I might hear what you're saying.

OMELET. One thickness of brick! What walls, you slut!

FYOKLA. Well, I didn't build 'em. Maybe that's the way they had to be. Blame the architect!

OMELET. The whole place is mortgaged. May devils devour you, you witch! *(He stamps his foot.)*

FYOKLA. You're a very ungrateful man. Anyone else'd be glad I took an interest in his welfare.

ANUTCHKIN. But, my dear Madam Fyokla, you did tell me she knew French. I think that was very wicked of you.

FYOKLA. She does too know French, she's been to school! She knows all them things: French, German, geography . . .

ANUTCHKIN. Madam Fyokla, you never heard her speak anything but Russian.

FYOKLA. What's wrong with Russian? *I* speak Russian. *You* speak Russian. The holy saints spoke Russian.

OMELET. Witch! She-devil! Wait till I get my hands on you!

FYOKLA. I'd just as soon not, sir. When it comes to woman beaters, I'd just as soon keep my distance.

OMELET. Woman beaters! *(He tries, unsuccessfully, to suppress his rage.)* Just you wait! I'll teach you to cheat honest men! And you can tell your precious Miss Agafya she's a bitch!

(Exit OMELET.)

FYOKLA *(to OMELET'S receding figure).* She says to tell you you're a son of one. *(To the others.)* Thinks he is somebody just 'cause he's fat as an elephant.

ANUTCHKIN. Now really, Madam Fyokla, much as it grieves me to have to say it, you are a deceiver, a wicked deceiver. You knew perfectly well that—if I'd known how Miss Agafya was educated—I should never have set foot in here. I have been grossly misled! Oh!

(Exit ANUTCHKIN.)

FYOKLA. Education's like vodka: you can easily take a drop too much. (KOTCHKAREV *laughs.)* What's eating you? (KOTCHKAREV *laughs, pointing at* FYOKLA.) He *is* a nut.

KOTCHKAREV *(through continuous laughter).* "How To Make a Marriage—by Madam Fyokla—queen of matchmakers"—matchmaker!—ha! ha! ha!

FYOKLA. When your father begot you he was "temporarily of unsound mind."

KOTCHKAREV *(still laughing his head off).* I shall split! I shall burst! (ZEVAKIN *starts to laugh with him.)* I shall die laughing! *(He sinks, exhausted, on a chair.)*

ZEVAKIN. I appreciate the mirthfulness of your disposition, sir. Reminds me of a midshipman in our squadron, name of Anton Ivanovitch. Most risible character, don't you know. You only had to shake your finger at him and he'd laugh for the rest of the day. It was catching too. You'd take a look at that fellow, and, by Jove, before you could say "yard arm," you'd be laughing yourself.

KOTCHKAREV *(just about recovered)*. Lord have mercy on us! The conceit of the woman! Now when I set out to make a marriage, I finish the job.

ZEVAKIN. *You* make marriages, Mr. Kotchkarev?

KOTCHKAREV. Certainly. I can marry anyone to anyone!

ZEVAKIN. The man I need, by God! Mr. Kotchkarev, marry me to Miss Agafya.

KOTCHKAREV. You? Why should *you* want to be married?

ZEVAKIN. That's rather an odd question, sir. Surely you know why people . . . it's an instinct . . . it's natural . . . even the animals and birds . . .

KOTCHKAREV. You just heard she has no dowry.

ZEVAKIN. That's a pity, of course. But money isn't everything, my good sir. The little woman's a charmer. She and I could get by without dowry—a tiny room . . . *(With his hands he indicates the dimensions of a cubicle)* . . . at the far end of a narrow landing, a bit of a screen for a wall . . .

KOTCHKAREV. Hey, you *like* her! *(Pause.)* You like her?

ZEVAKIN. She has flesh on her bones, you know. Never could stand a skeleton in skirts, no, sir. She's a fine figure of a woman.

KOTCHKAREV *(aside, looking at* ZEVAKIN). As for him, he looks like a tobacco pouch with no tobacco in it. *(Aloud.)* No, no, you mustn't get married on any account.

ZEVAKIN. What? Why not?

KOTCHKAREV. Well, for one thing, you're not good-looking enough.

ZEVAKIN. What!

KOTCHKAREV. She may be a fine figure of a woman, but you're not a fine figure of a man.

ZEVAKIN. By God, sir! Now you're being personal!

KOTCHKAREV. Because—between ourselves—I know you can take it. Because I know you want to know the truth. And, anyhow, I *will* marry you. To another lady.

ZEVAKIN. Another lady? No, no, sir. I must ask you to stick strictly to this one!

KOTCHKAREV. You absolutely insist?

ZEVAKIN. I absolutely insist. I . . .

KOTCHKAREV. Very good. I'll marry you to Miss Agafya—on one condition.

ZEVAKIN. Yes, yes?

KOTCHKAREV. That you leave it all to me.

ZEVAKIN. Leave it all to you? Getting married?

KOTCHKAREV. Getting engaged.

ZEVAKIN. At least I'll have to show myself to her!

KOTCHKAREV. Quite unnecessary. Go home, make yourself comfortable, and wait.

ZEVAKIN. Wait? How long?

KOTCHKAREV. How long? Oh, a little thing like this only takes me . . . a matter of hours.

ZEVAKIN *(rubbing his hands)*. That's great! But of course you need something in writing. My service record, my certificate for . . . She'll be making inquiries. Let me run and get my papers.

KOTCHKAREV. Also unnecessary, Mr. Zevakin. *(Taking him to the door.)* Go home, make yourself comfortable, and wait.

(Exit ZEVAKIN.*)*

What's happened to Podkolyossin? It certainly takes him a long time to fasten his trouser strap. I'd better look into it.

(Enter AGAFYA.*)*

AGAFYA *(looking round the room)*. The gentlemen have gone? Not one solitary gentleman left?

KOTCHKAREV. Not a one.

AGAFYA. I couldn't bear it, Mr. Kotchkarev. I was all of a tremble. That Mr. Omelet is a dreadful fellow. What beatings his wife will have to take! And I keep thinking he may be back at any minute.

KOTCHKAREV. Oh no, he mayn't. It's my personal opinion you'll never see Mr. Omelet again. Or Mr. Anutchkin, for that matter.

AGAFYA. How about Mr. Zevakin?

*(*ZEVAKIN *pops his head round the door.)*

ZEVAKIN *(aside).* I must hear what she says about me with that little rosebud of a mouth. I must!

KOTCHKAREV *(unaware of* ZEVAKIN'S *presence).* Who?

AGAFYA *(also unaware of* ZEVAKIN). Mr. Zevakin.

KOTCHKAREV. Oh, *him.* I couldn't believe you meant *him.* He's such an ass.

ZEVAKIN. What's this? What's this?

AGAFYA. He's rather nice-looking, Mr. Kotchkarev.

KOTCHKAREV. But he drinks. Like a fish, as a matter of fact.

ZEVAKIN. What? What?

AGAFYA. Of course, I couldn't marry a drunk.

KOTCHKAREV. It's worse than that. I couldn't give him a character reference of any kind.

ZEVAKIN *(aloud).* Now look here, Mr. Kotchkarev, you're speaking out of turn, by Jove! To appreciate my qualities is one thing —put in a word for me, sing my praises, don't you know—but, really, it's quite another to carry on this way. I begin to suspect you are no friend, sir. Who's not for us is against us, don't you know.

KOTCHKAREV *(aside).* Zevakin! What's *he* doing here? *(Aside to* AGAFYA.) Look at him. He can hardly stand, what did I tell you? You must give him his marching papers. *(Aside.)* Where in hell is Podkolyossin?

(Exit KOTCHKAREV.)

ZEVAKIN *(aside).* I see how it is. He promised he'd speak *for* me, then he goes and speaks *against* me. An eccentric! *(Aloud.)* Miss Agafya, I, um . . .

AGAFYA. Oh! I don't feel well! I have a headache!

ZEVAKIN. Which of us *doesn't* have his little defects, Miss Agafya? Look! *(He pulls the hair aside from the top of his head.)* See that? A bald patch. Only a small one. From fever on the high seas. With the squadron, you know. There'll be new hair on it soon, my barber guarantees it.

AGAFYA. I'm glad. I mean, sir, I couldn't care less.

ZEVAKIN. And, as for my complexion, it looks a lot better when I'm wearing black.

AGAFYA. I'm afraid I must leave you, sir. Oh, my head!

(*Exit* AGAFYA.)

ZEVAKIN (*as she leaves*). Leave me? But why, ma'am? What's wrong with me? Could you possibly maintain that my defects are more than superficial? (*The door bangs.*) Gone! It's happened again. Seventeen times this has happened to me. Seventeen! And always in the same way. Things go well for a while, then poof! the little skiff goes up in a cloud of smoke. They all refuse me. (*He paces the room, ruminating.*) My seventeenth refusal. And why? What is she after? What does she ask of life? And what possible objection . . .? (*He meditates.*) If I were disfigured, I could understand it, if I were even plain . . . (*He looks himself over.*) But, look at me, everything just exactly in place . . . Nature has showered her gifts upon me, don't you know. It's incomprehensible. Should I run home and see what I've got in my trunk? Though I have no furniture, I believe I have a poem in my trunk that no woman could resist. (*Pause.*) Incomprehensible. Went so well for a while. (*Pause.*) There's nothing for it, then. The old ship'll have to steer another course, that's all. What a shame!

(*Exit* ZEVAKIN. *Enter* PODKOLYOSSIN *and* KOTCHKAREV, *looking behind them.*)

KOTCHKAREV. He didn't even see us! And did he look sad!

PODKOLYOSSIN. You mean to say she refused him too?

KOTCHKAREV. Him too.

PODKOLYOSSIN. Y'know, I can't help feeling sorry for them. Damned embarrassing, to be refused.

KOTCHKAREV. Oh, damned embarrassing.

PODKOLYOSSIN. Still, I hardly believe she'd come right out and tell you she prefers me.

KOTCHKAREV. Prefers you? She adores you. She's in the grip of unbridled passion.

PODKOLYOSSIN. She said so?

KOTCHKAREV. She said the most amazing things. Talks of you all the time in the most extravagant language. Uses a thousand silly little terms of endearment. I'd blush to repeat them.

PODKOLYOSSIN (*smirking*). What does she call me? Lovey-Dovey? Popsy-Wopsy?

PODKOLYOSSIN. Let's see. Today's the eighth. Eight, nine, ten ... *(He counts on his fingers.)* The carnival's coming up in twenty-two days.

AGAFYA. Time just flies!

PODKOLYOSSIN. That's not counting today. *(Silence.)* Don't you admire the Russian worker?

AGAFYA. What?

PODKOLYOSSIN. The workers. Aren't they brave? The way they climb up on the roof—without turning a hair. I was passing a house this morning, there was a plasterer 'way up on top ...

AGAFYA. Oh? Where was that?

PODKOLYOSSIN. On my way to the office. *(Silence. The drumming starts again. Then* PODKOLYOSSIN *picks up his hat and bows.)*

AGAFYA. You're not leaving, Mr. Podkolyossin?

PODKOLYOSSIN. They say all good things come to an end. *(Pause.)* You'll forgive me for boring you?

AGAFYA. Boring me? Why, I'm having a lovely time!

PODKOLYOSSIN. No, no! I've been boring you.

AGAFYA. No, no! I enjoyed every moment of it!

PODKOLYOSSIN. Then, Miss Agafya, may I feel it might be all right for me to go so far as to suggest ... dropping in again sometime?

AGAFYA. But, Mr. Podkolyossin, you must. Please!

(They take leave. Exit PODKOLYOSSIN.)

AGAFYA. What an agreeable man! How nice to get to know him better! You can't help liking him, he's well behaved, and he has a good head on his shoulders, his friend was right. The only pity is, he's gone so soon. I wish he'd stayed a little longer, talking to him is so thrilling. He's no chatterbox. But, then again, *I'm* no chatterbox. I thought of several nice things to say to him, but I was too shy. My heart was pounding like a drum. A most agreeable man, I must go and tell Auntie!

(Exit AGAFYA. *Enter* PODKOLYOSSIN *and* KOTCHKAREV.)

KOTCHKAREV. What on earth are you going home for?

PODKOLYOSSIN. What on earth have I got to stay here for? I said it all.

KOTCHKAREV. You opened your heart to her?

PODKOLYOSSIN. Not that maybe. But everything else.

KOTCHKAREV. Not that? But the rest is nothing.

PODKOLYOSSIN. Now look here, old man, how could I just walk in, plonk myself down, and say: "We're getting married"?

KOTCHKAREV. You were closeted in with her a full half hour. What were you chattering about?

PODKOLYOSSIN. Miscellaneous subjects. It was rather pleasant. I enjoyed every moment of it.

KOTCHKAREV. You certainly like to run things close. One hour to the wedding, and you haven't proposed yet. You're still discussing miscellaneous subjects and having a pleasant time.

PODKOLYOSSIN. One hour to the wedding? What do you mean?

KOTCHKAREV. That's right. I've arranged everything.

PODKOLYOSSIN. The wedding—it's today?

KOTCHKAREV. That's right!

PODKOLYOSSIN. Today!

KOTCHKAREV. You told me you'd be ready as soon as the others were out of the way. Well, the others are out of the way.

PODKOLYOSSIN. And I'm a man of my word. Can't go back on my word, as it were. All I ask, my dear Kotchkarev, is a little respite. Say, a month or six weeks.

KOTCHKAREV. A month or six weeks?

PODKOLYOSSIN. Call it two months.

KOTCHKAREV. Are you crazy?

PODKOLYOSSIN. Six weeks, then.

KOTCHKAREV. Impossible. The small collation is on its way over. So, don't be pigheaded, Podkolyossin, get married!

PODKOLYOSSIN. I see your point. But I can't. I'm terribly sorry.

KOTCHKAREV. Can't? But you're a man, you can do what you set your mind on. Can't you?

PODKOLYOSSIN. Yes, later. Later, I really believe I could . . .

KOTCHKAREV *(an outburst)*. Oh, don't be so damned tiresome, you great slob!

PODKOLYOSSIN. Sorry, old man. But you must admit the situation is an awkward one.

KOTCHKAREV. What's awkward about it? It's time you took yourself in hand. Got a grip on yourself. Pulled yourself together. Exercised control. Ran your own life. . . . Do I make myself approximately clear?

PODKOLYOSSIN. I follow you. I see what you're driving at. If it were at all possible—if only to please you—

KOTCHKAREV. Podkolyossin, must I go down on my knees before you?

PODKOLYOSSIN. What for?

KOTCHKAREV. I must! I do! *(And he does.)* I'm on my knees before you, I beg, entreat, implore, and conjure you. Don't be pigheaded!

PODKOLYOSSIN. I say!

KOTCHKAREV *(angrily getting up)*. You bastard!

PODKOLYOSSIN. Curse away! Don't mind me!

KOTCHKAREV. You're so silly. The conclusion is borne in upon me with a certain tragic inevitability that you are the silliest man that ever lived.

PODKOLYOSSIN. Go on, go on. Let yourself go!

KOTCHKAREV. Why have I gone to all this trouble? For what? For whom? For you, you blithering idiot. I give you up.

PODKOLYOSSIN. That sounds like a good idea. Do that. Give me up.

KOTCHKAREV. The trouble is, without me you'll never amount to anything. If I don't get you married, you'll be a blithering idiot for life.

PODKOLYOSSIN. I see what you mean, old man. But why should I bother you so much?

KOTCHKAREV. Because I've taken it as my mission to reform you.

PODKOLYOSSIN. Write it down Mission Not Accomplished.

KOTCHKAREV. Oh, go away!

PODKOLYOSSIN. Yes. I rather think I shall.

KOTCHKAREV. I hope you enjoy the drive.

PODKOLYOSSIN. Yes. I think I shall.

KOTCHKAREV. I hope you break your neck in a traffic smash.
Drunken cabbie. Gruesome collision. Your torso transfixed by
the shaft. Podkolyossin, it's all over between us. Don't let me
ever see your face again.

PODKOLYOSSIN. No. That's right. I think I shan't.

(Exit PODKOLYOSSIN.)

KOTCHKAREV. And my best to your old friend the devil! *(He
opens the door and shouts after him.)* Idiot! *(Paces the room in
agitation.)* Idiot! And *I'm* not much better. Am I? Another
idiot. What have I been working so hard for? Shouting till I'm
hoarse? What is he to me—a long-lost cousin? What am I to
him—a wet nurse? A fairy godmother? Why do I trouble myself with him? Why? Why do we do any of the things we do?
Why not wish the devil joy of him? The crook! I don't like his
face! I could tweak his nose, I could box his ears! *(He does so,
in the air.)* Now what riles me is the way I let him walk right off
the lot. He just walks away, goes off home, curls up on the
couch, and smokes his pipe, the nasty creature! Of all the faces
I don't like, he has the nastiest, I couldn't think up a nastier one
if I were God. I know what I'll do. I'll bring him back! I
simply won't let him run out on us. I'll bring him right back!

(Exit KOTCHKAREV, *running.)*

(Pause. Enter AGAFYA.)

AGAFYA. My heart is still pounding. Wherever I turn, there, in my
path, stands Mr. Podkolyossin. There is no escaping your destiny, they say. I begin to understand the saying. I try to get my
mind off him. I wind wool. I do a little embroidery. But no:
Mr. Podkolyossin springs out at me from the shadows.
(Pause.) Maiden innocence, adieu! They will come for me, lead
me to the church, hand me to this man, leave me alone with him,
ooh! It makes me shudder. *(She is weeping now.)* Girlhood
and peace, farewell, and welcome, trouble! Children are
trouble. Little boys quarrel all the time, and little girls get to be
big girls before you can turn round, and then husbands have to
be found for them. May their husbands be *good* men, that's all!
If they marry gamblers and drunks, I won't be able to bear it.
My daughters married to . . .! Oh! *(The weeping sets in*

again.) It isn't as if I've been single very long. Barely twenty-seven years. I hadn't even got around to enjoying the single state ... *(With a change of tone.)* But where is Mr. Podkolyossin? Why the delay?

(Enter PODKOLYOSSIN, *pushed through the door by* KOTCH-KAREV.)*

PODKOLYOSSIN *(stammering)*. Miss Agafya, I've come back ...

AGAFYA. So I see, Mr. Podkolyossin.

PODKOLYOSSIN. I've come back just to explain ... one small thing. But I rather think you'll find it strange, won't you?

AGAFYA *(lowering her eyes)*. What is it, Mr. Podkolyossin?

PODKOLYOSSIN. Oh, you'll find it strange. Won't you?

AGAFYA *(her eyes still lowered)*. I don't know what it is yet, Mr. Podkolyossin.

PODKOLYOSSIN. But, when you do, don't you think you'll find it strange?

AGAFYA *(with a gulp)*. No, I don't! I'm sure anything you say will be very nice!

PODKOLYOSSIN. But ... this is something you haven't heard yet. (AGAFYA *lowers her eyes still more.* KOTCHKAREV *comes forward and stands at* PODKOLYOSSIN'S *shoulder.*) It's this. *(Pause.)* No, no, I'll tell you some other time.

AGAFYA. Tell me what, Mr. Podkolyossin?

PODKOLYOSSIN. Well, actually, Miss Agafya, I meant to tell you without more ado, as it were. The words don't come out, somehow.

KOTCHKAREV *(aside, folding his arms)*. This is not a man, it's a scarecrow, it's a satire on man, it's an old woman's old slipper.

AGAFYA. Why won't they come out, Mr. Podkolyossin?

PODKOLYOSSIN. Why? I wish I knew, Miss Agafya. *(Suddenly fluent.)* Maybe at heart I'm a skeptic. Incapable of faith. Or maybe I'm horribly abnormal, a morbid personality not worthy to tie your ...

KOTCHKAREV *(aloud)*. Enough of this monkey business. Miss Agafya, the mysterious message is that Mr. Podkolyossin can't live another hour without you. Night and day he is haunted by your beauty, et cetera. Will you marry him?

PODKOLYOSSIN *(almost in panic, aside to* KOTCHKAREV, *nudging him).* This is extremely irregular, my dear fellow!

KOTCHKAREV *(going right on).* So what do you say, Miss Agafya? Will you consent to make him happy, et cetera?

AGAFYA. A girl should not presume to say her little love can make a big man happy. But I consent.

KOTCHKAREV. Then it's a deal. Congratulations! Give me a couple of hands.

(PODKOLYOSSIN *tries to whisper in his ear.* KOTCHKAREV *frowns and shakes his fist.* PODKOLYOSSIN *gives his hand.)*

KOTCHKAREV *(joining their hands).* Praise God from Whom all blessings flow, I hereby authorize this marriage, and thereunto set my seal. Marriage, if you ask my opinion, marriage is . . . well, it's not like calling a cab and taking a bit of a ride. No, it's different, it's a sacred duty. Someday, when I have the time, I'll tell you just *how* sacred and how much of a duty. For now, kiss the bride. Yes, you may. In fact, you must. (AGAFYA *lowers her eyes.)* Yes, Miss Agafya, in accordance with time-honored custom, I'm afraid you must let him kiss you.

PODKOLYOSSIN. Yes. Yes, that's right, you must. You must let me kiss you, ma'am! *(Very gingerly, he kisses her.)* What a nice little hand you have, Miss Agafya. Why? Why do you have such a nice little hand? I, um, wish the wedding to take place forthwith! At once!

AGAFYA. At once? Oh? As soon as that?

PODKOLYOSSIN. Sooner! Enough of this shilly-shallying! I want to get hitched this very minute!

KOTCHKAREV. That's the spirit! Bravo! You'd better hurry and get dressed, ma'am. I've sent for the carriage. As a matter of fact, I've invited the guests too. They're on their way to church. Your wedding dress is ready?

AGAFYA. Just give me one second, Mr. Kotchkarev.

(Exit AGAFYA.)

PODKOLYOSSIN. Kotchkarev, I'd like to say thank you. Just a simple thank you from the very depths of my soul, as it were. You've taught me what the word friendship means. Next spring I shall undoubtedly visit your father's grave.

KOTCHKAREV. Not at all, my boy, I'm very happy for you. *(He kisses him on both cheeks.)* May your marriage bed be blessed with plenteous offspring!

PODKOLYOSSIN. Ah, sweet mystery of life, at last I've found thee. A new world is opening before me. I see it germinating, bubbling, effervescing. Until now, I didn't even notice, it was all there, and I didn't see it! I didn't see myself, old man. Just went on from day to day in a dull and monotonous round of meaningless meandering. Understood nothing!

KOTCHKAREV. Life begins on the other side of despair. Or someplace. Let me see if the food's all here, I'll be right back. *(Aside.)* But it might be just as well to hide his hat.

(Exit KOTCHKAREV, *taking* PODKOLYOSSIN'S *hat.)*

PODKOLYOSSIN *(lost in thought).* I understood nothing! A bachelor's life *is* nothing, a man might just as well be dead. Life —what has it been for me? Getting from one day to the next, trailing to the office, grinding away at a desk, guzzling my dinner, snoring in my sleep. Frivolous! Banal! To live unmarried is not to live at all. If I were the Tsar, I'd order everyone married at once, I'd abolish bachelordom overnight. *(Pause.)* The thought of getting married! The idea that one will be married in a matter of minutes! In the twinkling of an eye, to taste the ecstasy of fairy tale and romance! Hm. *(He mops his brow.)* Of course, it has its thorny side. Say what you will, it's rather alarming, once you let your mind dwell on it. To bind yourself—for life. No retreat, no retraction. You're goosecooked. It's too late even now. My fate is irrevocably sealed. The carriage is outside. In a few minutes I'll be in church, the ceremony will have begun ... My fate is sealed. Irrevocably? Irrevocably. I couldn't even get through that door without them all pouncing on me. "Where are you going? What for?" How about the window? No, that's absurd. It *is* rather temptingly open, though. No, no, it's undignified. And much too high up. *(Moves over to the window.)* Well, actually, it's not as high as all that, a fellow's done bigger jumps than that in his time. Where's my hat? Vanished? That settles it. I never go out without a hat. *(Pause.)* Not that I'm adamant on the point. We're never too old to learn. *(Again he pauses. Then on a sudden impulse, he hops onto the window ledge.)* Without a hat be it. God's will be done! *(He jumps out the window. His*

voice is heard from the street outside. He sounds knocked out.)
Holy Moses, what a drop! Hey, cabby!

CABBY'S VOICE. Yes, sir? Where to, sir?

PODKOLYOSSIN. Kanavka. Near the Semyonovsky bridge.

CABBY. It'll cost you ten kopecks, sir.

PODKOLYOSSIN. In the circumstances, it's a bargain. Drive on!

(The cab is heard rattling off. Enter AGAFYA, *timidly, in her wedding dress, hanging her head.)*

AGAFYA. What is the matter with me, I wonder? I'm all of a tremble again. And I feel shy! Wouldn't it be nice if he weren't here, if he'd slipped out for something? *(Looking round, timidly.)* He *isn't* here! Where is he? Where can he have gone? *(Opening the door, and speaking into the hallway.)* Fyokla, where's Mr. Podkolyossin? Has he gone out?

FYOKLA'S VOICE. He's in there, miss, he's in there!

AGAFYA. In where?

(Enter FYOKLA.)

FYOKLA. Sitting right here.

AGAFYA. Where?

FYOKLA. That's funny. He didn't come out. I was in the hallway the whole time.

AGAFYA. Where can he be?

FYOKLA. Could he have gone out by the back stairs? Is he with your aunt?

AGAFYA. Aunt Arina! Aunt Arina!

(Enter ARINA *in her best clothes.)*

ARINA. What is it, my dear?

AGAFYA. Have you seen Mr. Podkolyossin?

ARINA. No, my dear. I thought he was here.

FYOKLA. Well, he's not! And he didn't come out the door!

AGAFYA. Well, he isn't here.

(Enter KOTCHKAREV.)

KOTCHKAREV. Is anything wrong?

AGAFYA. Yes. We've lost Mr. Podkolyossin.

KOTCHKAREV. Lost him? How could you lose him in here? Where's he gone?

AGAFYA. He hasn't gone.

KOTCHKAREV. Not here and not gone?

FYOKLA. That's right. He's not here. But he hasn't left the room. I was sitting right outside the door.

ARINA. And *I* know he didn't leave by the back stairs.

KOTCHKAREV. Well, he can't be lost if he never got out. He must be hiding. Now, Podkolyossin, don't be a fool! Come out! Give yourself up! You won't be shot, we'll let you off with a life sentence, the priest is all ready to pronounce a verdict! *(He looks behind the cupboard, glances under the chairs.)* Well now, that's rather baffling. He couldn't possibly have gone out, his hat is still in the next room, and he never goes out without hat, trust me to think of everything.

ARINA. Anyhow, Dunyashka would know, she was out in the street. Dunyashka!

(Enter DUNYASHKA.)

Dunyashka, have you seen Mr. Podkolyossin? We've lost him.

DUNYASHKA. Mr. Podkolyossin? Oh yes, ma'am, he jumped down from the window five minutes ago. (AGAFYA *shrieks and clasps her hands.)*

ALL THREE. The window!

DUNYASHKA. That's right, ma'am. Then he got into a cab and drove off.

ARINA. Dunyashka, are you telling the truth?

KOTCHKAREV. No, she's not, she's lying. The thing is impossible.

DUNYASHKA. No ma'am, no, sir, ask the man at the general store if you don't believe me. He saw him too. Ten kopecks the cabby charged him.

ARINA *(going to* KOTCHKAREV). So you'd make sport of us, would you? This is your idea of a joke? Well, you may be a gentleman, but, let me tell you, sir, you're a crook for all that. I'm no lady, but I'd die before I'd do such things. *(To* AGAFYA.) Come along, my dear, have a good cry, my dear, and when you've cried your heart out, we'll invite the merchant Starikov to come and drink tea with us.

(Exit ARINA, *taking* AGAFYA *with her.* KOTCHKAREV *is stunned.)*

(Pause.)

FYOKLA. We-e-ll! So this is our smooth operator! This is the man who can make marriages better than a matchmaker! Ha! Some of the gentlemen on my list may not be the cream of the cream, but I certainly never had no window jumpers, no, sir.

KOTCHKAREV. The thing is absolutely impossible. I know: I'll bring him back!

(Exit KOTCHKAREV.)

FYOKLA *(calling after him).* A lot you know about getting folks married! *(To the audience.)* When a man just walks out, something can always be fixed up. But when a bridegroom jumps out the window, the marriage don't so easily come back in at the door.

FROM A MADMAN'S DIARY

a monologue

This is actually a series of monologues, each monologue consisting of the "madman's" diary entry for that day. In performance, the actor can be reading each entry back to himself just after he has written it.

Place:

St. Petersburg

Time:

The Eighteen Thirties

October 3rd. Extraordinary thing happened today. I got up late. When Mavra brought in my boots, newly shined, it was after ten. If I'd known the sour look I'd get from my Department Head, I wouldn't have gone to the office at all. "You rush around like a madman," he's been saying lately, "the Devil himself couldn't bring order into the chaos you make, starting paragraphs with small letters, leaving out the date." It was pouring, so I took my umbrella. On the street saw our Director's carriage draw up in front of a store. Could *he* be *here*? No, out *she* fluttered from the carriage like a little bird, eyes and eyebrows flashing past me, looking first right, then left ... God in Heaven, I thought, I'm lost, I'm lost forever! And *her*, venturing out in weather like this! Don't tell me women aren't crazy about clothes. She didn't spot me. I muffled myself up because my overcoat was so filthy and old-fashioned. Her dog didn't quite make it into the store behind her but got left out

on the street. I'd seen it before. Fancy French name: Fidèle.*
And I heard a voice say, "Hi, Fidèle," a minute later. Two ladies
passed, one old, one young, under an umbrella. Then, that voice.
"Shame on you, Fidèle!" I now saw Fidèle was sniffing a little dog
that was following the ladies. And I saw her—the dogs were both
ladies too—mouth these words: "I've been (bark) very sick (bark)."
I *was* surprised to learn that Fidèle talked. Staggered. But amaze-
ment wore off when I recalled the recent report from England of a
fish that came to the surface and uttered two words in a language so
strange the scholars have racked their brains for three years to figure
it out, so far unsuccessfully. It was also in the papers that two cows
went into a store and ordered a pound of tea. The startling thing
was to hear Fidèle say: "I *wrote* to you, Madge. Evidently Polkan
didn't deliver my letter." Never heard of a dog that could *write*.
Takes a nobleman to write properly. The lower orders leave out the
commas and periods. They have no idea of style . . . Seems I've
been seeing and hearing things lately that I never saw or heard
before. So I said to myself, "I'd better follow Madge and find out
more about Sophie." I did. Until the two ladies stopped in front of
a large house, which I recognized. Zverkov's house. A dump.
Everyone lives there. Cooks, foreigners, civil servants. Like dogs,
one on top of another. A friend of mine who's an accomplished
trumpet player lives there. The ladies went up to the fifth floor.

******

October 4th. Got to the Director's house early. Started sharpening
the Director's quill pens right away. Seeing me do that makes my
Department Head jealous. The Director's quite a scholar. All those
books he has. Not even in Russian. In French. German . . .
Very serious man. As I hand him some papers, he'll say: "how's
the weather?" "Damp," I'll say, "damp." He likes me. If only his
daughter . . . Noticed it was after 12:30, and the Director hadn't

---

*In the original, the two dogs of the story are called Madgie and Fidèle in that
order. "Fidèle" is moderately snobbish being French, "Madgie" is doubly snobbish being English. Simon Karlinsky who pointed all this out to me also suggested reversing the names since, in English, "Fidèle" will do something toward
suggesting snobbery, while "Madge" will do nothing at all. I rejected Mad*gie* as
less English-sounding than plain Madge. "Chère Madge," or "Madge ma chère,"
is absurd, but Gogol never put up much of a fight against absurdity.

even left his bedroom. 2:30: the door opens, is it he? Holy
Fathers, it's *her*! And what a dress, white like a swan! It's like
suddenly the sun came out. "Has Papa been here?" What a voice,
the voice of a canary! "Excellency," I didn't say this but I thought
it, "don't have me put to death or, if you must, let it be by your very
own hand!" What I did say was, "No, Ma'am." She looked at me.
She looked at the books. She dropped her handkerchief. I leaped at
it, slipped on the damn parquet floor, nearly bust my nose, regained
my balance, picked up the handkerchief. What a lovely one, the
very smell proved it belonged to a general's daughter. Never mind,
never mind, silence. Worked on for another hour and left. Once
home, lay on my bed a long time. In the evening walked over to the
Director's house, and waited a long time outside. She didn't come
out.

******

November 6th. My Department Head made me furious. "I know
you've been running after the Director's daughter, and what are
you? A zero. Nobody. Just look in the mirror." Oh well, he's
jealous. Sees I get better treatment. Doesn't realize I'm a gentleman. And I could get promotion. I'm only 42. It's just that I'm
short of money.

******

November 9th. Left for office at 8. Department Head pretends he
didn't see me come in. We act complete strangers. Sort out documents. Leave at 4. Pass Director's house. No one in, apparently.
Lay on bed most of evening.

******

November 11th. Sharpened 23 quill pens in Director's study. For
him—and her. Four for her. Wish I knew what went on in higher
circles. Talking with him, I get as far as, "it's cold," "it's warm,"
and stick. I'd love to get into the drawing room. The door is ajar
sometimes, and from there I can see another door leading to another
room. What luxury! The china! The mirrors! I'd love to see
where she . . . her boudoir, jars, bottles, flowers so delicate you
can't breathe on them. Her dress. More air than matter. One peek
into her bedroom. Paradise. The stool where her little foot lights as

she gets out of bed. Over the tiny foot, the snowy white stocking. Ooh! Never mind, never mind, silence. Something dawned on me today. That conversation on Nevsky Avenue between the two dogs. What I need is the letters that passed between those two dirty dogs. I almost did summon Fidèle and ask her point blank: "About the young lady. Tell me all." But dogs are smarter than people. She could have talked. She just didn't want to. Very well, tomorrow, I go over to the Zverkovs and cross-examine Madge. With any luck I'll get my hands on the letters Fidèle sent her.

******

November 12th. Reached the sixth floor, rang the bell, pretty girl came to the door. Same girl I'd seen with the old lady. When she blushed I realized she needed a boyfriend, poor little thing. "I've got to talk with your dog," I said. She didn't take it in. Too stupid. But Madge came out and barked at me, and when I tried to take hold of her, nearly sank her teeth in my nose. I spotted her basket in the corner, rushed over, rummaged around in the straw and, to my great joy, pulled out a bundle of papers. Seeing which, the dirty dog bit me on the thigh. When she found I'd taken the papers, she started whining and fawning on me. I said, "No, my dear, goodbye!" and took to my heels. The girl looked scared. Must've thought I was mad. Back home, couldn't work on the papers, because Mavra decided the floor needed washing. *I* decided to take a walk and have a good think. Yes, I would now learn what this whole drama amounted to, the letters would tell all. "Dogs are smart," I said to myself, "even the Director's private life will be dealt with. Even something about hers, but, sh!" Towards evening, I returned home, and spent most of the time lying on my bed.

******

November 13th. The letter is quite legible, though the handwriting is slightly doggy. "Dear Madge, your name is a little bit vulgar. Like Rosie" Correct punctuation too. Even my Department Head doesn't write this well and he boasts of having gone to a university. "My mistress, whom Papa calls Sophie . . ." Sh! "Papa's a strange man. Doesn't often even speak, but a week ago kept saying to himself: 'Shall I get it, shall I get it?' Even turned to me and asked: 'Shall I get it, Fidèle?' I sniffed his shoes and left the room. Then, ma chère, about a week later he came home all smiles. And

men in uniform kept coming and congratulating him on something.
Papa was more chipper than ever during dinner, and kept lifting me
shoulder-high to ask me: 'What's that, Fidèle? Look!' Some bit of
ribbon on his lapel. I did sniff, but it had no smell. Licked it too.
It was salty." Ah, so Papa is ambitious. "Today, Sophie..."
Sophie! "... was all excited, dressing for a ball. Don't see why
people dress. Why can't they go around without, as we do? It's
nice. Don't know what she sees in them, personally, balls. Gets
home at six in the morning all pale and thin, I can tell they don't feed
her there. I like to eat woodcock in sauce or wing of roast
chicken.." The style is so jumpy. Not human. Doggy. Let's
see another letter. No date on this, either. "I have many suitors,
and you couldn't imagine how ugly some of them are. But there is
one gallant, name of Trésor, and, my dear, you should see his little
snout..." What trash. Fancy filling a letter with stuff like this.
And it's not dogs my soul pines for, it's human beings. I demand
human interest. Skip a page. "Sophie was sitting there sewing. A
footman enters and announces: 'Teplov.' Sophie throws her arms
round me and cries: 'Ask him in.' 'Oh, Fidèle' says she, "he's a
Gentleman of the Chamber, dark hair, black fiery eyes!' She ran to
her room. A young man with black sideburns came in, smoothed
his hair in the mirror, and looked around. I growled and settled
down by the window. Sophie re-enters. She curtseys, he clicks his
heels. They then talked rubbish. You know, about some lady at a
ball who got the dance wrong, and someone called Lidina who
thought she had blue eyes when they were green. How can one
compare this young courtier with Trèsor with his delicate snout and
a white spot on his brow? I don't know what she sees in him. She
might just as well go for that fellow in Papa's office. A civil
servant, ugly as a tortoise in a sack. With a funny name. Sharpens
quills all the time. Has hair like hay." What's this? Hair like hay?
Me? "Sophie can't look at him without laughing." That's a lie.
You're jealous, dog. And I know who's behind it: my Department
Head. He hates me. One letter left, let's seek enlightenment there.
"Madge, ma chère, excuse the delay, it's been a time of heavenly
rapture. Sophie is in love. The courtier comes every day. Rumor
has it there'll be wedding bells. Papa is in high spirits. A Gentleman of the Chamber is just what Papa wanted for her..." Some-
times I wish I was a Gentleman of the Chamber. Or a general.
Then she'd be mine. And I'd see all these other chaps crawling

before me. I could tell'em to go to hell. Ach! It's enough to make
you cry. I tore that dumb little dog's letter to pieces.

******

December 3rd. Does a Gentleman of the Chamber have a third eye
in the middle of his forehead? Is his nose made of gold? I have a
title: Councillor, ninth grade in the bureaucratic structure. There are
fourteen grades. But there could have been a mistake. Like when a
serf discovers he was really a lord all along. I'm no serf. I'm of
gentle birth. I might discover I'm a general. An epaulette on my left
shoulder. A blue sash across my chest. Then she'd sing a tune. As
would her dear Pop, that ambitious man. I could also be promoted.
To Governor General, for instance.

******

December 5th. Reading the papers all morning. Strange happen-
ings in Spain. The throne is vacant, and the nobility are having
trouble choosing an heir. They're thinking of choosing Donna
Somebody. Some Donna. They can't have that, can they? They
need a king. They say there is no one. But there must be. To gov-
ern. Where's he hiding? *Why's* he hiding? Family reasons? A
foreign threat? France?

******

December 8th. For various reasons, did not get to the office today.
Couldn't get that Spanish business out of my head. A Donna on the
throne? They wouldn't permit it. For one thing England would
never stand for it, and how about the Austrian Emperor and the Tsar
of all our Russias? Mavra said I was absentminded at supper: I
threw two plates on the floor, and they broke. After dinner I walked
along a street going downhill: didn't learn much from that.* Lay
on my bed afterwards for a long time, pondering the Spanish
question.

******

---

*Prince Mirsky's translation reads: " . . . went to look at the mountains but
did not find them helpful."

April 43rd, 2000 A.D. A day of triumph. There is a king of Spain.
At last he has been found. It's me. Came to me in a flash only
today. How could I ever have imagined I was a Councillor? Crazy.
Though it's nice no one thought of putting me away. Now all is
clear. Before, it was misty. The reason being that people think the
brain is located in the head. Wrong. It is carried by the wind from
the Caspian Sea. The first thing I did was tell Mavra. When she
heard that the person before her was the King of Spain, she nearly
dropped dead. She'd obviously never seen the King of Spain
before. I was big about it. Convinced her the new sovereign was
well-disposed towards her, and if sometimes she made a mess of
my shoes, I didn't mind. Didn't get to the office today. To hell
with them. My friends, I have had enough copying your filthy
documents.

******

86th Martober, between day and night. One of the clerks stopped
by, saying it was time I went to the office, I hadn't been there for
three weeks. Just for a joke, I went. The head clerk thought I'd
bow and apologize. Actually I gave him a cool look—not hostile
but not really friendly. Sat down at my desk as though no one else
existed. They put some papers in front of me. I was supposed to
work on them. Didn't lift a finger. Brouhaha. The Director is
coming! The clerks bow. Not me. They button their jackets. Not
me. Director, is he? Know what he really is? A cork. An ordinary
cork—used for stopping up bottles. They gave me a paper to sign.
Expecting to see "Clerk Number So-and-So" at the bottom of the
page. But, higher up, where the Director puts his name, I signed:
"Ferdinand VIII." Religious silence. "No need for a show of loyalty," said I, and stalked out. Went straight to the Director's house.
He wasn't there. The footman wouldn't let me in at first, so I said
something that made his arms drop to his side, limp. Went right to
her boudoir. She was sitting in front of the mirror. I didn't tell her
I was King of Spain. Just remarked that unimaginable happiness
awaited her—despite all the evil plots against us both. Thinking that
should be enough, I left. But women are crafty, and only then did it
dawn on me who they're in love with. They are in love with the
Devil. I'm not kidding. See the woman with the lorgnette on the
other side of the theatre? Think she's looking at the fat man with the
medal? She isn't. She's looking at the Devil just behind him. And

now the Devil's hiding inside the medal and beckoning. She'll marry him, that's for sure. And those clerks, pretending to be such patriots when all they're after is money, for which they would sell their own mother! Such ambition is caused by a little bubble under the tongue containing a tiny worm the size of a pinhead and all the work of some barber from Gorokhovaya Street. I forget his name but, with the help of an old midwife, he intends to spread Mohammedanism throughout the world. Has already converted most of France.

******

No date, this day didn't have one. Walked incognito down Nevsky Avenue. The Tsar drove past. Everyone, including me, took his hat off. I wasn't ready to reveal my identity. For that, I have to be presented at Court. What has stopped me so far is having no royal clothes. Tailors are such rascals, so corrupt. Decided to make a mantle out of my new uniform. Make it myself. Shut in my room so no one can see. Had to cut up the uniform with the scissors.

******

Don't remember the date. There wasn't any month either. Damned if I know what to make of this. Cloak now ready. I put it on. Mavra screamed. Shall I present myself at Court? Can't go on my own, and the Spanish deputation hasn't arrived. But they will, any minute.

******

The first. What can have held them up? France? Went to the post office about it.

******

Madrid, 30th Februarius. Am in Spain now. It happened with extraordinary speed. The Spanish deputation arrived this morning. The carriage went at such a pace, we were at the Spanish frontier in half an hour. But then there are railroads all over Europe now. And trains go very fast too. Strange place, Spain. In the first room I saw, there were a lot of people with shaven heads. Grandees? Soldiers? Old Spanish custom? The way the Lord High Chancellor treated me was strange. Shoved me into a little room and said: 'Call

yourself King of Spain one more time, and I'll beat the bejesus out
of ya.' I knew this was just a test, so I called myself King of Spain
right off, whereupon the Chancellor hit me. Hard. Twice. In the
back. The test was: could I bear in mind I was being knighted and
keep from crying out? I did. I passed! Left on my own, got down
to government business. I've discovered something: China and
Spain are the same country. Check it out. Try writing "Spain":
you'll find you've written "China." I'm really sore about this thing
that is going to happen at 7 tomorrow. The earth is going to crush
the moon. An account has been written by Wellington—the English
chemist. I don't think the moon can take it. Too delicate. Made in
Hamburg, usually. The English should do something about it.
From tarred rope and olive oil. What a stink! The moon is too fra-
gile for people to live on. Only noses live there. Seen your nose
lately? Of course not. It's on the moon. When the earth lands
there, our noses are going to be ground into the moon's surface. I
put on my socks and shoes and rushed into the state council chamber to tell the police to stop the earth falling on the moon. I was
getting a lot of help from the grandees with shaven heads when in
came that Chancellor with his stick and hit me. Drove me back to
the little room. Oh, the strength of tradition in Spain!

******

January in the same year which came after February. Still, I don't
really understand Spanish customs. They shaved *my* head today. I
shrieked. Told them *I* didn't want to be a monk! They dripped cold
water on my head. Don't recall just what happened then. It was
hell. They could hardly hold me down, I was in such a frenzy.
What customs! The kings must have been really dumb not to have
abolished these customs. I know: I must've fallen into the hands of
the Inquisition. That "Chancellor" must've been the Grand Inquisitor. But how can kings be subject to the Inquisition? Is France
behind this? With England lurking in the background? They say
when England takes snuff, France sneezes.

******

The 25th. The Grand Inquisitor was here. Hearing his footsteps, I
hid under the table. Not finding me in, he called out: "Poprishchin!" I didn't say a word. "Aksenty, son of Ivan Poprischin!
Councillor! Nobleman!" I still didn't answer. "Ferdinand VIII,

King of Spain!" At that I almost popped out, then thought better of
it, I didn't want any more cold water on my head. He spotted me all
the same, and got me out from under the table with that stick, which
hurts like crazy. However, I made a discovery today. I found out
that every rooster has a Spain. Know where? Right under the tail
feathers.

******

ht 34 eht Mth yrae February 349. I can't stand it any more. Good
God, what are they doing? They're dripping water on my head.
They will not hear, they will not look, they will not listen. Why?
What do they want? What can I give them when I have nothing?
My head is burning. Everything is spinning round. Save me. Take
me away. Give me a troika with horses swift as the wind! Up on
your box, driver, let the bells ring! Soar, horses, carry me out of
this world. The sky is billowing ahead of me. A little star in the
distance. The forest rushes by, the crescent moon among its trees.
A guitar is heard through the mist. The sea is on one side. On the
other, Italy. Russian peasant huts over there. Is that my home, blue
in the distance? Is that my mother at her window? Save your son,
Mother, shed a tear on his aching head, they are tormenting him,
there is no place for him in the whole wide world, they are hunting
him down. Mother! Have pity on your sick little boy! . . . And
did you all know this: Hussein Pasha of Algiers has a wart right
under his nose?*

---

*Vladimir Nabokov has translated the last phrase: "a round lump growing right
under his nose." David Magarshack writes: "Originally he [Gogol] finished his
story with the remark, 'The French King has a boil under his nose' (the Russian
word *shishka*, a boil, is also used colloquially for 'trouble', and the sentence
could therefore also mean, 'The French King is in the devil of a mess', a
reference to the abdication of Charles X in 1830). But the abdication of a king
after a revolution being a rather dangerous subject, Gogol altered it to, 'The Bey
of Algiers has a boil under his nose,' a reference to the deposition by the French
in 1830 of the last Bey of Algiers, Hussein Pasha." In correspondence with the
present editor, Simon Karlinsky strongly dissents from Magarshack's view
. . . Wart, lump, or boil? Prince Mirsky translates: wen.

INSPECTOR

A Comedy in Five Acts
by
Nikolai Gogol

If your face is lopsided, don't blame the mirror.
— Russian proverb

РЕВИЗОРЪ

КОМЕДІЯ,

ВЪ ПЯТИ ДѢЙСТВІЯХЪ

соч. **Н. ГОГОЛЯ.**

———◆———

САНКТПЕТЕРБУРГЪ,

ПЕЧАТАНО ВЪ ТИПОГРАФІИ А. ПЛЮШАРА.

——◆——

1836.

Inspector: Title page (1836)

Characters:

   The GOVERNOR *of the Town*
   The GOVERNOR'S WIFE
   MARYA, *his daughter*
   MISHKA, *his young servant*

   SUPERINTENDENT OF SCHOOLS
   JUDGE
   DIRECTOR OF CHARITIES
   POSTMASTER
   DISTRICT DOCTOR
   POLICE CHIEF
   SVISTUNOV, *a local cop*

   PYOTR IVANOVITCH BOBCHINSKY, *landowner*
   PYOTR IVANOVITCH DOBCHINSKY, *landowner*

   HLESTAKOV, *a clerk from St. Petersburg*
   OSSIP, *his servant, middle aged*
   ABDUL and other SHOPKEEPERS
   SERGEANT'S WIDOW
   LOCKSMITH'S WIFE

   A WAITER *at the inn*

   A GENDARME *from St. Petersburg*

(This is a cast of twenty plus shopkeepers. But the same actor can play the Doctor, the Waiter, and the Gendarme; and other doubling is possible.)

Time:

   The Eighteen Thirties

Place:

   A small town in provincial Russia

Gogol's notes on characters and costumes, translated by Arthur A. Sykes and Constance Garnett.

The GOVERNOR *is a man who has grown old in the state service—in style and manner, a smart official. He wears an air of dignified respectability, but is by no means incorruptible. He speaks to the point, generally avoiding extremes, but sometimes launching into an argument. His features are harsh and stern, like those of a chinóvnik [functionary] who has worked his way up from the lowest rank. His coarse and ill-educated nature causes him to pass with rapidity from fear to joy, and from servility to arrogance. He is dressed in uniform with loops and facings, and wears Hessian boots with spurs.*

Anna Andreyevna, the GOVERNOR'S WIFE, *is still tolerably young, and a provincial coquette, brought up on novels and albums and household trivialities. She is very inquisitive, and displays now and then a vain disposition. Henpecks and ridicules her husband to a certain extent on minor points, when she can get the best of him in argument. Changes her dress four times in the course of the piece.*

HLESTAKOV *is a young man, about twenty-three years old, mean and insignificant to look at. Not overburdened with common sense, being, as they say, "without a tsar in his head." He would be designated as "very frivolous" in the government offices. Speaks and acts without reflection, and lacks concentration. His style of address is abrupt, and his remarks are totally unexpected. (The actor should sustain this role with the greatest possible naiveté.) Dresses in the latest fashion.**

OSSIP, *his servant, resembles other middle-aged persons of his class. Talks seriously, looks downwards, and is fond of arguing and lecturing his master. He scarcely varies the tone of his voice, addressing Hlestakov bluntly and even rudely. He is the cleverer of the two, and sees through things quicker; is silent and uncommunicative, and a rogue. Wears a rather worn-out overcoat of a gray or blue color.*

---

*Gogol has more to say about Hlestakov in his letters. Perhaps he suspected that the role would usually be misinterpreted as it still is in the late 20th Century. See especially pages 55 and 165 of *Letters of Nikolai Gogol,* Selected and Edited by Carl R. Proffer. Ann Arbor, Michigan, 1967.

BOBCHINSKY *and* DOBCHINSKY *are short, fat, inquisitive, and remarkably like each other. They both wear short waistcoats, and speak rapidly, with an excessive amount of gesticulation. Dobchinsky is the taller and steadier, Bobchinsky the more free and easy, of the pair.*

Lyapkin-Tyapkin, the JUDGE, *has read five or six books, and so is somewhat of a freethinker. He is very fond of philosophic speculation, carefully weighing each word. (The player should be careful to preserve a judicial and consequential style.) Speaks with a bass voice and a prolonged drawl, clearing his throat beforehand, like an old-fashioned clock, which buzzes before it strikes.*

Zemlyanika, the CHARITY COMMISSIONER, *is very fat, slow, and awkward; nevertheless an intriguing rascal, most obliging and officious.*

The POSTMASTER *is an artless simpleton.*

The other characters do not need special explanation; their prototypes are continually before us.

The actors must pay special attention to the last scene. The last word ought to give an electric shock to all present at once. The whole group ought to change its position instantly. A cry of astonishment ought to spring from all the women as though from one bosom. Disregard of these instructions may ruin the whole effect.

ACT ONE

A room in the Governor's House. Double doors in the center, smaller doors at the sides. The GOVERNOR, the DIRECTOR OF CHARITIES, the SUPERINTENDENT OF SCHOOLS, the JUDGE, the DOCTOR, and, at the door, SVISTUNOV, a local cop.*

GOVERNOR. I have called you together, gentlemen, to give you a distinctly unpleasant piece of news. A Government Inspector is on his way from Petersburg.

DIRECTOR OF CHARITIES. A Government Inspector?

GOVERNOR *(raising his hand)*. A Government Inspector. With secret instructions.

JUDGE. A Government Inspector?

GOVERNOR. Travelling incognito.

JUDGE. I'll be damned.

DIRECTOR OF CHARITIES. And things have been nice and quiet so long.

SUPERINTENDENT OF SCHOOLS. Secret instructions.

GOVERNOR. I've felt it coming on. Guess what I dreamt of all last night. Rats. A pair of most unusual rats. Black, both of 'em, and unnaturally large. They came in; sniffed; then ran out. *(Pause.)* I'd better read you the letter I've received from Hmikov. *(To the Director of Charities:)* You know Hmikov. Ahem. "Dear friend and benefactor . . ." *(He looks ahead to the real "meat" of the letter, mumbling some of the words:)* "To inform you . . ." Yes. "Hasten to inform you that a government official has been sent from Petersburg to inspect the province in general and our district in particular. I have this from reliable sources. But he pretends to be a private person. Now since, like everyone else, you sometimes cut a few corners—if something falls into your hands, you don't give it away—" *(Pause.)* Oh well, we're all friends here. "I advise you to take

---

*Gogol's three cops have been reduced to one in this version.

certain precautions. The man may arrive any moment if indeed he hasn't arrived already and is staying unobserved somewhere in town. Only yesterday I—" Oh, the rest is family stuff: "My sister Anne is here on a visit with her husband who has got fat but plays the violin . . ." So there we are.

JUDGE. Extraordinary. Very. What's behind it?

SUPERINTENDENT OF SCHOOLS. Yes. What's this all about? Why a Government Inspector?

GOVERNOR. Why, indeed? How about Fate? Maybe it's Fate. *(He sighs.)* It always happened to the other towns, not to us.

JUDGE. So there must be a reason. Politics! The country on the point of war. The government sends someone to check out our loyalty.

GOVERNOR. Are we anywhere near the frontier? *Any* frontier? Ride a racehorse in any direction from here, it'd take you three years to get to a foreign country.

JUDGE. That's irrelevant. The government would have something in mind. It makes no difference that we're in the sticks. Because the government would argue—

GOVERNOR. Well, in any case, I've warned you, gentlemen. And I've already taken care of *my* neck of the woods: will *you* take care of yours? *(To the Director of Charities:)* That includes you. There's nothing the Inspector will more want to see—oh yes, *en passant,* if you like—than our, shall we say? charitable institutions. Your territory, ha? Can you make that hospital look halfway decent? Put some clean robes on the patients? Generally make the place look less like a blacksmith's shop?

DIRECTOR OF CHARITIES. No problem. Clean robes. Right.

GOVERNOR. With the patient's case history on a card at the head of the bed? In Latin? Better still, Greek? *(Turning to the District Doctor:)* But that's your department, Doctor. Patient's name. Day, month, year when admitted. Yes, I know you dose them with strong tobacco, but must one sneeze one's head off the minute one sets foot in the place? And there are too many patients. That will be attributed to bad management. Or, *are you listening now?* to the inefficiency of the Doctor.

DIRECTOR OF CHARITIES *(taking the Doctor's arm).* But none of your fancy prescriptions, Dr. Huebner, give nature a chance!

These are just people: if they're gonna kick the bucket, they'll kick it anyway; if not, not. *(To the others:)* How could our friend *(he pats the Doctor on the arm)* advise them anyway, he doesn't know Russian?

DISTRICT DOCTOR. Deutsch. Deu—*(Barely audible to begin with, his voice drops to zero.)*

GOVERNOR *(to the JUDGE).* As for you, Judge, check out the law court. That hallway where people come with their complaints and petitions, must it always be full of geese? One falls over them. Yes, I know, geese are a good thing, and these belong to your porters. But it's not proper in a public place. *(As the JUDGE starts to interpose:)* Why didn't I say so before? It's something I forgot.

JUDGE. The geese will be transferred to my kitchen. Want to come to dinner?

GOVERNOR. And it looks bad to have the laundry out to dry in the courtroom. Ragged old clothes at that. And the closet full of legal papers. Why a hunting crop outside? I *know* you love hunting, but wouldn't it be better to take the crop away—just for a time?—You can put it back once the Inspector's gone. And your clerk, yes, I know he's a Legal Beagle, but he smells of vodka. Yes, I know he says that's his natural smell. I don't care. There are such things as de-odorants. How about onions? Garlic, then? Or could the Doctor here give him a pill?

DISTRICT DOCTOR *(in German).* Was? Wa—*(Again his voice fades out.)*

JUDGE. No. The clerk says that's just how it is. His nurse let him drop when he was little, and he's smelled of vodka ever since.

GOVERNOR. Oh, well, I was just thinking . . . about what goes on in court . . . that which Hmikov calls "cutting corners." What can I say? Let him that is without sin, etcetera. God's will be done, we don't care what atheists think, etcetera . . .

JUDGE. There are sins and sins, *I* say. I for example openly admit taking bribes, but what bribes? Just pups. German shepherds. They don't count, do they?

GOVERNOR. Certainly they do. Bribery is bribery.

JUDGE. Not at all. Now if a man takes a fur coat for his wife, and it's worth—

GOVERNOR. So what if you only take pups? You're an atheist. *I* go to church every Sunday, but you make my flesh creep with what you say about the creation of the world.

JUDGE. I think! I'm a freethinker!

GOVERNOR. You think too much. But never mind, God will take care of the courthouse somehow, and *he* won't even notice the place. It's you *(turning to the Superintendent of Schools)* that must look out, being in charge of all our teachers. Oh, I know they've had a college education. That doesn't stop them being a queer lot. There's the one—what's his name again?—the one with the fat face who goes like this *(he grimaces),* then lifts his beard from under his tie, and carefully smooths it out. Pulling a face at one of the boys wouldn't matter so much, it may even be necessary, I don't know, but supposing he does it at . . . our Visitor, and our Visitor takes it personally? That could lead anywhere!

SUPERINTENDENT OF SCHOOLS. What can I do? I've talked to him about it. Just the other day, when a Very Important Person visited the class, he pulled that face. Pulled it and pulled it. With the best of intentions, of course. But speaking of freethinkers, I got a talking to from that Person about freethinking teachers and their unsettling effect on the young.

GOVERNOR. And your history teacher. Clever fellow, I don't deny that. Erudite. But the man lets his feelings run away with him. I heard one of his lectures. As long as he stayed with the Assyrians and Babylonians, it wasn't so bad, but when he came to Alexander the Great, I thought the house was on fire. He jumped up, took hold of a chair, and smashed it on the floor like this. *(He imitates the moves.)* Now I know Alexander was a very great hero but why smash the furniture? The government had to buy a new chair.

SUPERINTENDENT OF SCHOOLS. He's excitable. I've told him so more than once. "Say what you like," he replies, "but in the cause of education I am ready to give my life."

GOVERNOR. Gifted people are either alcoholic or they pull faces at you.

SUPERINTENDENT OF SCHOOLS. I wouldn't wish an education on my worst enemy. In our educational system, each teacher lives in dread of the other. Each one gets in the other's way. Each one wants to show off.

GOVERNOR. All of which wouldn't matter except *he*'ll be incognito. "So there you all are," he'll say of a sudden, "which one is the Judge?" "Lyapkin-Tyapkin." "Bring him over! And who is Director of Charities?" "Zemlyanika." "Bring him over."

POSTMASTER *(entering)*. What's this, gentlemen? A certain person is on his way here?

GOVERNOR. You haven't heard, Mr. Postmaster?

POSTMASTER. I *have* heard. From Bobchinsky. He just stopped by at the post office.

GOVERNOR. Well, what do you think?

POSTMASTER. Think? That it's war! With Turkey!

JUDGE. My opinion precisely.

GOVERNOR. Both of you are crazy.

POSTMASTER. War with Turkey! And all the fault of the French!

GOVERNOR. *We're* gonna catch it, not the Turks. I have a letter.

POSTMASTER. A letter? That's different.

GOVERNOR. So where do you stand now?

POSTMASTER. Who cares where *I* stand? *You're* the Governor.

GOVERNOR. Where do *I* stand? Well, I'm a little afraid. Not afraid. Uneasy. About our shopkeepers. They get mad at me. They say I'm on the take. Now that's not fair. If I ever accept anything it's strictly without prejudice. But I wonder *(taking the Postmaster by the arm, to one side)* if someone hasn't been telling tales out of school. Do something for me. Unseal and read every letter at the post office, coming or going. To catch a possible tattle tale. When you find no evidence, re-seal the envelope. Or just leave it open.

POSTMASTER. I already do that. Not as a security measure. It's just that I'm curious. I like to know what goes on. It's fun, too. I even learn a lot. More than in The Moscow News.

GOVERNOR. All right then. Have you read anything about that Person from Petersburg?

POSTMASTER. Nothing about Petersburg. A lot about Saratov. And Kostroma. And Parts East. You'd love some of the letters. Wonderful descriptions. There was a lieutenant the other day, describing a ball. He compared it to Elysium: girls, bands playing, banners flying . . . I have it on me. Like to hear it?

GOVERNOR. This is not the moment. But if you come upon any complaint, or any reports on our life here, would you hold them for me?

POSTMASTER. Delighted.

JUDGE. But be careful. You might get into trouble.

POSTMASTER. Oh, well!

GOVERNOR. Nonsense. It would be different if it were all public. But this is strictly private.

JUDGE. Still, trouble does seem to be brewing. I myself came here intending to give you a present right now. A pup. Sister to the pup aforementioned. I felt I could afford it. Chaptovitch is suing Varkovinsky: a suit that can last the rest of my life. Meanwhile, I can hunt on the estates of both . . .!

GOVERNOR. Damn your hunting. What about that incognito? At any moment, the door may open and in will walk—

(*Enter* BOBCHINSKY *and* DOBCHINSKY.)

BOBCHINSKY. Something extraordinary has occurred.

DOBCHINSKY. Something surprising has happened.

ALL. What? What can it be?

DOBCHINSKY. Something quite unforeseen. We get to the inn—

BOBCHINSKY. Pyotr Ivanovitch and myself get to the inn—

DOBCHINSKY. Pardon me, Pyotr Ivanovitch, I'm telling this story.

BOBCHINSKY. No, no, allow me . . . you'll never find the words . . .

DOBCHINSKY. You'll get mixed up and forget.

BOBCHINSKY. No, I won't, let me tell it. Gentlemen, tell him not to interfere.

GOVERNOR. But what has happened? Tell us, for goodness' sake, or I'll have a heart attack. Sit down, gentlemen! (*They all sit around the two Pyotr Ivanovitches.*) Now, what *is* it?

BOBCHINSKY. I shall begin at the beginning. As soon as I left you—you'd received that letter and seemed quite worried about it—I ran—Please don't interrupt, Pyotr Ivanovitch, I know what I'm saying.—I ran to Korobkin's. Not at home. Ran to

Rastakovsky's.* Not at home. Ran to the post office. Told the Postmaster here the news you'd received. Then I met Pyotr Ivanovitch here—

DOBCHINSKY. Near the spot where they sell hot pies.

BOBCHINSKY *(nodding)*. Where they sell hot pies. Seeing Pyotr Ivanovitch, I said: "Have you heard what the Governor has learned from reliable sources?" And he had: from your *(to the Governor)* housekeeper. She'd gone to Pochechuev's house, I don't know for what—

DOBCHINSKY. Some French brandy.

BOBCHINSKY. A keg of French brandy. We were on our way to Pochechuev's. Don't interrupt, Pyotr Ivanovitch. And Pyotr Ivanovitch said: "Let's go to the inn, it's my tummy. Nothing to eat all day. My tummy." Pyotr Ivanovitch's tummy. "They have fresh salmon," he went on, "we can have lunch." No sooner had we entered the inn than a young man—

DOBCHINSKY. Not bad appearance. Civilian dress.

BOBCHINSKY. Not bad appearance. Civilian dress. Strolled through the room looking very imposing. Such carriage! Such a lot going on upstairs! *(He points to his head)* "More here than meets the eye," I said to Pyotr Ivanovitch, who'd already contacted Vlass, the innkeeper. His wife's time was up just three weeks ago, a boy, in great shape, he'll be an innkeeper like his father before him. "Who," says Pyotr Ivanovitch, "is that young man?" "That," says Vlass . . . Pyotr Ivanovitch, don't interrupt, you don't know how to tell this story, you lisp, it's your teeth, the one tooth anyway . . . "That young man," says Vlass, "is an official from Petersburg, by name, Ivan Alexandrovitch Hlestakov. He's on his way to Saratov but behaving strangely. Been at the inn nearly two weeks without paying a kopeck. Living on credit." Then it dawned on me and I said: "Aha!"

DOBCHINSKY. *I* said: "Aha!"

---

*The Russian original brings Korobkin and Rastakovsky on stage in Act Five.

BOBCHINSKY. But then I said it too. "Aha!" we both cried, "but why would he stay here if he's on his way to Saratov?" Obviously, he's your Person from Petersburg.

GOVERNOR. What Person from Petersburg?

BOBCHINSKY. The Government Inspector.

GOVERNOR. It can't be.

DOBCHINSKY. Who else? He has a travel pass for Saratov. He doesn't *go* to Saratov. And he doesn't pay his bill.

BOBCHINSKY. It's him all right. A professional investigator. Takes *note* of everything. Noticed we were eating fresh salmon—on account of his tummy, *(pointing to the other Pyotr Ivanovitch)* remember?—He positively *peered* at that salmon.

GOVERNOR. Lord have mercy, what's his room number?

DOBCHINSKY. Five. Under the stairs.

BOBCHINSKY. Number five! The room where those officers had their fight last year!

GOVERNOR. He's been there a long time?

DOBCHINSKY. Two weeks.

GOVERNOR. Saints above, get me out of this! During those two weeks, the sergeant's widow has been flogged, the prison inmates haven't had their proper rations, the streets have been in an uproar, and two feet deep in filth and litter. Oh my poor head! *(He clutches it.)*

DIRECTOR OF CHARITIES. So what do you think, Governor? Shall we all proceed in a body to the inn?

JUDGE. Let's observe protocol. Clergy and business people first. The book says—

GOVERNOR. No, no, let me decide. I have proved master of the situation before this. God was often on my side. A young man, you say?

BOBCHINSKY *(nodding)*. Not more than twenty-four.

GOVERNOR. So far, so good. Not some old devil. Young and manageable. Very well, gentlemen, each to his own department. I'll make a private visit to the inn—will you come with me, Dobchinsky?—just to make sure the person from Petersburg is being taken care of. *(To the* COP *at the door:)* You.

COP. Yessir?

GOVERNOR. Send someone for the Police Chief, then come right back.

(Exit COP.)

DIRECTOR OF CHARITIES. I agree with you, Judge: trouble brewing.

JUDGE. Not for you. Clean robes on your patients and you've nothing to worry about.

DIRECTOR OF CHARITIES. It's the food. The smell. They're all supposed to be on clear consommé but the whole place reeks of cabbage.

JUDGE. Well, *I'm* not worried. A Person from Petersburg won't be interested in a mere district court. And if he does glance at some legal document, he won't understand it. Solomon himself couldn't understand our documents. I've been on the bench fifteen years but, as for legal papers, I take one look and throw them in the waste basket. *(As they go out, the* JUDGE, *the* DIRECTOR OF CHARITIES, *the* SUPERINTENDENT OF SCHOOLS, *and the* POSTMASTER *collide in the doorway with the* COP.)

GOVERNOR. Carriage ready?

COP. Yessir.

GOVERNOR. Aren't you bringing me some more cops? How about Prohorov?

COP. Drunk. And completely out of it. Two buckets of water in his face and he still didn't come to.

GOVERNOR. O my God! Then go out and—No, I know, bring me my sword—and my new hat. *(COP leaves. To Dobchinsky:)* Let's go.

BOBCHINSKY. Me too, me too.

GOVERNOR. The carriage won't hold three.

BOBCHINSKY. Oh, I can trot along behind, then stay and just peek through the keyhole. I want to see what the Person does—

(The COP *returns with a hatbox and a sword.)*

GOVERNOR *(taking the sword).* Get me some more cops. Then —But look at this sword, scratched! And just think, that Abdul, the Merchant, could easily spare me a new one! No respect! They're all the same, our shopkeepers, interested in nothing but complaints and petitions! Now, about the cops, have each one take a street, I mean take a broom, and street a sweep! Sweep a street. *(The* COP *laughs.)* I know about you, Svistunov. You sweep the silver right off the table and into those boots of yours, and don't think I don't notice! When that shopkeeper offered you two yards of broadcloth for your uniform, you swiped the whole bolt. I noticed. The bribes you're taking are way above what's due to a man of humble station: I noticed that too.

(He waves the COP *off. Enter the* POLICE CHIEF.*)*

GOVERNOR *(ironically)*. Ah, his honor the Police Chief. Where were *you* hiding out?

POLICE CHIEF. Nowhere. I was right here at your gate.

GOVERNOR. That Person from Petersburg has arrived, and what have you done about it?

POLICE CHIEF. Followed your instructions. Sent my cops to clean up the streets.

GOVERNOR. Which cops? Derzhimorda?

POLICE CHIEF. Nah. He's on fire engine duty.

GOVERNOR. Prohorov is drunk.

POLICE CHIEF. As a lord.

GOVERNOR. Well, how come you let that happen?

POLICE CHIEF. I didn't. There was a brawl. Prohorov was sent to handle it. He came back high as a kite.

GOVERNOR. Hm. Putovitzin. Tallest cop in town. Put *him* on the bridge. That'll look good. Next: where the shoemaker lives— break up that old fence. Make a mess with the pieces. When there's lots of demolition, a Person can tell the town is humming, public works in preparation, etcetera. *(Takes hat out of hatbox and puts it down.)* But, O dear, I was forgetting all that garbage by the fence. Forty cartloads of the shit. This town is a dump, Chief: you put up a fence—or a monument to one of our great men—and the place is used to dump garbage. Oh yes, and get the word around: If the Person from Petersburg asks the workers if they're satisfied, they're to say: "Yes, your honor." Just like that, "Yes, your honor." It isn't a long speech to learn. And if they say they're *dis*satisfied—tell 'em this—I'll give 'em something to be dissatisfied *with* afterwards! *(Picks up hatbox in mistake for hat and starts praying:)* O God, end our sufferings soon and I'll buy you a bigger candle than you ever saw!

soldier will tell you about army life. Or explain which star is
which in the sky. Then a lady's maid may put in an appearance . . . *(He rolls his eyes.)* Anyway, it's . . . civiliza-
tion. You're treated right. You're called Mister. When you're
tired you hail a cab and there you sit like a lord. True, maybe
you don't have the fare, in which case you tell the cabby you're
going indoors for the money, then you go indoors and don't
come out again . . . In Petersburg there's always a way.
Well, nearly always. You eat good. Some of the time. Other
times you starve. Like here. Which is his fault. What can we
do about *him?* His pop sends him money but it slips through his
fingers. *He* always takes cabs. Theatre tickets every day. Then
after a week or so, he's broke and has to start selling off his
clothes. He was stark naked under his coat and pants one time:
he'd sold his shirts and underwear. Sells at such a loss. A hundred ruble coat goes for fifteen, the pants are almost given away.
And why? Why? He doesn't like work. Instead of going to the
office, he likes to promenade on Nevsky Avenue. Or play
cards. If his old man ever found out! It wouldn't help him any
that he's in government service, his old man would rip his pants
off and beat his ass. *(Pause.)* Here, the situation is, they won't
send any more food to this room till we've paid for what we've
already had. And I'm so hungry I could eat the whole world.

(He stands up, hearing his master coming. Enter HLESTAKOV,
holding out his hat and cane.)

HLESTAKOV *(when* OSSIP *does nothing).* Aren't you going to take
these? *(*OSSIP *takes them.)* The bed is all mussed up.

OSSIP. It is?

HLESTAKOV. Lolling on *my* bed.

OSSIP. Why would I do a thing like that?

HLESTAKOV *(pacing the room).* Any tobacco in that jar?

OSSIP. You had the last of it four days ago.

HLESTAKOV *(stopping the pacing, loudly).* Ossip!

OSSIP. Sir?

HLESTAKOV *(less firmly).* I want you to go downstairs.

OSSIP. Where downstairs?

HLESTAKOV *(less firmly still).* The kitchen. *(Shakily:)* Order some
food.

OSSIP. I'd rather not.

HLESTAKOV. You're disobeying me?

OSSIP. No food till you pay up. *They'll* disobey you.

HLESTAKOV. How dare they?

OSSIP. The landlord says he'll tell the Governor. He called us names.

HLESTAKOV. What names?

OSSIP. Oh, I dunno: swindlers, rogues, rascals, cheats, scoundrels . . .

HLESTAKOV. How dare you use such language to me?

OSSIP. He says he'll lodge a formal complaint, and we'll end up in jail.

HLESTAKOV. You must talk to him.

OSSIP. I better have him come and talk to you, sir.

HLESTAKOV. What would *I* want with a coarse creature like that?

OSSIP. Sir—

HLESTAKOV. All right, I can take a hint. Summon the landlord! *(Exit* OSSIP. HLESTAKOV *talks to himself.)* It's disgusting how hungry I am. I took a stroll on the theory that my appetite would wear off. It didn't. But for that spree at Penza, there'd have been enough money to get home on. That infantry captain did for me. Piled up trick on trick, and cleaned me out in fifteen minutes. I'd like just one more game with him . . . What a rotten little hick town this is! Nothing on credit even from the greengrocer's! They're mean!! *(Whistles something from* Robert the Devil, *followed by the Russian folksong* Red Gown,* *then something nondescript.)* Looks like the landlord won't come up.

(Enter OSSIP *with a* WAITER.*)*

Robert the Devil is the then popular opera by Meyerbeer: Hlestakov will mention it in Act III. Though it would be easy to insert in Gogol's text titles familiar to a late 20th-century audience, the titles he cites, known or unknown now, have been kept, so as not to disturb the illusion that we are in the Russia of the Eighteen Thirties. This note applies also to the list of musical and literary items in Act III though, there, two titles are still current today: Mozart's *Marriage of Figaro* and Bellini's *Norma.*

WAITER. The landlord wants to know what he can do for you, sir.

HLESTAKOV. Oh, good morning, my friend, and how are *you?*

WAITER. Very well, thanks.

HLESTAKOV. How are things going at the inn?

WAITER. Very well, thanks.

HLESTAKOV. Many guests?

WAITER. Quite a few.

HLESTAKOV. Well, my friend, they haven't brought my dinner up yet, would you tell them to hurry? I have an appointment.

WAITER. The landlord says he won't send it up. He's gonna lodge a complaint with the Governor.

HLESTAKOV. About what? Think it out. I've got to eat, right? Must eat or I'll waste away.

WAITER. He says he won't send any more food till you've paid for what you've had.

HLESTAKOV. I know. But reason with him.

WAITER. What'll I say?

HLESTAKOV. Well, as I say, that a man must eat, that money is one thing but—I know: maybe a peasant like him can go without food for a day, even two days, but a gentleman . . . Something along that line.

WAITER. All right.

(He and OSSIP *go out.)*

HLESTAKOV *(to himself)*. This really isn't fair. I'm hungrier than I've ever been. Is there any money to be raised on what clothes I have left? My pants? But I must arrive home in my Petersburg suit. Pity they wouldn't let me have a carriage on credit from Yokhim's. Then I could've returned to Petersburg *en carrosse,* lamps all lit, Ossip in livery perched up behind, stopping by, like one of the nobs, at some distinguished neighbor's, the footman announcing: "Ivan Alexandrovitch Hlestakov, gentleman, of Petersburg, wishes to know if you're receiving, sir." Here in the sticks they don't even know the expression: "receiving." When some peasant comes to see them, he pushes his way into the drawing room like a bear. . . . Once in, I head straight for the daughter of the family, "Enchanté, mademoiselle!" *(He does some bowing and scraping and rubbing of his hands, then the fantasy blows away.)* Ugh. *(He spits.)* I'm so hungry I'm sick to the stomach.

(Re-enter OSSIP.*)*

HLESTAKOV. Yes?

OSSIP. Your dinner, sir.

(Enter the WAITER *with food.)*

HLESTAKOV *(jumping up in his chair).* Dinner! Hooray!

WAITER *(unloading his tray).* The landlord says this is definitely the last time.

HLESTAKOV. The landlord? I spit on the landlord! What's that you've got?

WAITER. Soup and beef.

HLESTAKOV. That's it? Soup and beef?

WAITER. That's it, sir.

HLESTAKOV. It's not enough. Ask him what he means by it.

WAITER. He says it's too much.

HLESTAKOV. No sauce even?

WAITER. There isn't any.

HLESTAKOV. How could that be? I looked in the kitchen myself. They were preparing all manner of dishes. And in the dining room two little men were munching smoked salmon and all sorts of goodies.

WAITER. Well, there is and there isn't.

HLESTAKOV. Explain yourself.

WAITER. There isn't.

HLESTAKOV. Cutlets? Fish?

WAITER. For gentlemen as pays, there *is.*

HLESTAKOV. You're a fool.

WAITER. Yessir.

HLESTAKOV. You're a pig. If *they* can have it, *I* can have it: that's common sense. I'm a traveller, they are travellers.

WAITER. No, sir, that's not right.

HLESTAKOV. Not right?

WAITER. No, sir, they pay up.

HLESTAKOV. There's no arguing with an idiot. *(He tastes the soup.)* This is not soup, it's water. It may stink, but it has no taste. Take it away.

WAITER. I can take it away, sir, but the landlord says: "If he doesn't like it, he can lump it."

HLESTAKOV *(stopping him from taking the soup away).* Don't be familiar with me, my man, keep your hands off *my* dinner. *(Has more soup.)* My God. *(Another mouthful.)* This *must* be chicken soup, there are feathers floating in it. *(Another mouthful.)* All right, let's try the beef. Ossip, you finish the soup. *(OSSIP does so.)* Call this beef?

WAITER. Yessir.

HLESTAKOV. It's cast iron. No knife can cut it. *(Nonetheless he has cut a slice. He tries to chew it.)* My jaws just aren't strong enough, I'd need a chopping machine, it's breaking my teeth. *(He swallows.)* So that was beef, I'll take your word for it. Now: dessert!

WAITER. There ain't none.

HLESTAKOV. No sauce. No dessert. This is highway robbery. *(With the help of OSSIP, the WAITER has cleared the table. The two go out. HLESTAKOV again talks to himself.)* So I get just enough to make me even hungrier. If I had one kopeck I'd send Ossip out for a bun.

OSSIP *(re-entering).* The Governor of the town is here. Asking for you, sir.

HLESTAKOV *(alarmed).* What?!—That damn landlord has—The Governor's gonna haul me to jail? Can I carry this off like a *grand seigneur*—in my tumbril *en route* for the guillotine? I doubt it. As ill luck will have it, I've already made a pass at a shopkeeper's daughter in this town . . . I won't go, though! Who the hell does he think I am—a shopkeeper—a laborer? I know how to handle *him*. *(He stands tall.)* How dare you, sir? I simply won't have it!!

(The door handle turns. HLESTAKOV turns pale and shrinks. Enter the GOVERNOR with DOBCHINSKY: they both stand still. HLESTAKOV and the GOVERNOR look at each other in alarm, then the GOVERNOR pulls himself together.)

GOVERNOR *(standing at attention)*. Sir, I humbly hope you are well.

HLESTAKOV *(bowing)*. My respects to you, good sir.

GOVERNOR. You will have to excuse the intrusion—

HLESTAKOV. Pray don't mention it, good sir.

GOVERNOR. But it is my duty as Governor to see that visitors to our town—distinguished visitors—suffer no inconvenience . . .

HLESTAKOV *(faltering at first but then gathering confidence)*. Well, what can I do? It's not my fault . . . I really *am* gonna pay . . . Money will come in from . . . home. *(BOBCHINSKY peeps in at the door.)* The innkeeper's to blame, sending me beef hard as iron and soup with God knows what in it: I had to throw it out the window. The man's been starving me for days. Even the tea is "off," it smells of fish, so, actually, why should I . . .?

GOVERNOR *(intimidated)*. Please forgive me, sir. It's really not my fault. There's good beef on the market—from Kholmogori . . . Where does *he* get his beef from? In any case, if anything at all is not . . . as it should be, I will certainly take you elsewhere.

HLESTAKOV *(jumping)*. No! I won't go! "Elsewhere" indeed! You mean jail, and I know it, how dare you, sir? Did you know I am in government service in Petersburg? Know what I'm gonna do—?

GOVERNOR *(to himself)*. Merciful God, what a violent man, and he's found out everything, he must've been talking to our damned shopkeepers.

HLESTAKOV *(bluffing aggressively)*. You can bring a regiment here, I won't go with you. I'm going to write to *the Minister* in Petersburg! *(He bangs his fist on the table.)*

GOVERNOR *(still at attention but trembling now)*. It was just my inexperience, sir. And they don't pay me enough. My salary hardly covers tea and sugar. So, yes, I've taken bribes, sir. But such small ones. Cloth for a suit. A bottle of wine for my table. And the sergeant's widow, with the store, it's not true I had her flogged, that's a lie circulated by my enemies. They stop at nothing.

HLESTAKOV. But I've had nothing to do with them! *(Pause.)* I don't even know why you mention them. Or the sergeant's widow, for that matter. As to flogging me, I dare you! That's a big job! Besides, what's wrong? I'll pay up. I'll pay up. I just don't happen to have the cash on me. That's why I'm staying on. I haven't a kopeck.

GOVERNOR *(to himself)*. Artful devil. Putting us off the scent, ha? How to get at him? Must try something, and what will be will be. *(To him:)* If it's money you need—or anything else for that matter—I'm entirely at your service, sir. It's my duty as Governor.

HLESTAKOV. Yeah, lend me some money. I'll pay the landlord pronto. Two hundred rubles. Or less.

GOVERNOR *(producing the bills)*. Here's two hundred. You needn't count it.

HLESTAKOV *(taking the money)*. I'm much obliged. I'll return it the minute I'm on my country estate. I was caught short, you know. But you're a real gentleman. That changes everything.

GOVERNOR *(to himself)*. Thank God he took it. All should be plain sailing now. I slipped him four hundred.

HLESTAKOV. Ossip! *(Ossip comes in.)* Bring the waiter. *(Ossip leaves. To the* GOVERNOR *and* DOBCHINSKY:*)* But please be seated, both of you.

GOVERNOR. No, no. We don't mind standing.

HLESTAKOV. Please! I see it now. You are straightforward. You are hospitable. And here was I thinking you'd come here to— Please sit down.

*(*GOVERNOR *and* DOBCHINSKY *sit.* BOBCHINSKY *peeps in at the door and listens.)*

GOVERNOR *(to himself)*. If he wants to be incognito so be it. We'll cooperate. Pretend we have no idea who he is. *(To him:)* As I was saying, we came to the inn—this is Pyotr Ivanovitch Dobchinsky—a local landowner—in the normal discharge of our duties. We always take care that distinguished visitors are properly treated. Some governors wouldn't give a damn but Christian benevolence prompts me to make sure our visitors are well entertained. This time, I am amply rewarded by the agreeable acquaintance thereby made.

HLESTAKOV. Well, I'm as pleased as you are. But for you I was slated to stay here indefinitely. How could I *ever* have paid up?

GOVERNOR *(to himself)*. What a story! *Him* penniless? *(To him:)* May one make so bold as to enquire whither you are bound?

HLESTAKOV. My family's estate in the Saratov province.

GOVERNOR *(to himself, ironically)*. And he doesn't even blush. I shall have to watch my step. *(To him:)* Travel is so interesting, isn't it? There's a lot of delay, changing horses, and so on, but what a diversion for the mind. You *are* travelling for pleasure?

HLESTAKOV. No. Father sent for me. He's furious because I haven't got my promotion in the Civil Service. He thinks they give you the Order of Vladimir the day you arrive in Petersburg. He's never seen the inside of a government building.

GOVERNOR *(to himself)*. His father now. What yarns he can spin! *(To him:)* Will you stay long in Saratov?

HLESTAKOV. Who can tell? Father is stupid, you see, stubborn as a mule, but I'm gonna tell him I can't live without my Petersburg. Shall I waste away among peasants? My soul craves culture.

GOVERNOR *(to himself)*. One lie after another. But not much, physically: I could knock him over with a feather. Hm. I think I know how to make him talk turkey. *(To him:)* Everything you say is true. Here in the sticks one can't even sleep at night. One gives one's all for one's country and for what? Recognition? Zero. *(Looks round.)* Isn't this room rather damp?

HLESTAKOV. And full of bugs that bite like dogs.

GOVERNOR. That such a cultured visitor should suffer from little creatures unworthy even to exist! It's rather dark, too, isn't it?

HLESTAKOV. Very dark. The landlord refuses to provide candles. And you know, sometimes a man wants to do something. Read, say. Or even write. Well, I can't. It's too dark.

GOVERNOR. May I then venture to ask ... but no, I'm not worthy.

HLESTAKOV. What?

GOVERNOR. I'm not worthy.

HLESTAKOV. Of what?

GOVERNOR. There is a room in my own home, light, quiet, would you . . .? But no, I'm not worthy of the honor. Please don't be offended.

HLESTAKOV. I shall be delighted.

GOVERNOR. Really? Then *I* shall be delighted. And my wife will be overjoyed. Hospitality first, I always say, especially when one's visitor is a man of culture. And that's not flattery. I speak from the heart.

HLESTAKOV. Thank you. Just like me. Can't *stand* insincerity.

(Enter the WAITER *with* OSSIP. BOBCHINSKY *peeps in.)*

WAITER. Yes, sir?

HLESTAKOV. Give me the bill.

WAITER. I gave it to you this morning. For the second time.

HLESTAKOV. I'm supposed to remember such things? How much is it?

WAITER. The first day, one full dinner. Second day, smoked salmon. Thereafter—

HLESTAKOV. Don't itemize everything. Just give me the total.

GOVERNOR. Don't trouble your head about it, sir. *(To the* WAITER, *waving him out of the room:)* I'll take care of this.

HLESTAKOV *(putting the money back in his pocket).* Thank you.

*(*BOBCHINSKY *peeps in.)*

GOVERNOR. Now perhaps you'd like to see some of our local institutions?

HLESTAKOV. Really? Like what?

GOVERNOR. Oh, I just thought you might want to know how we . . . our management of, um—

HLESTAKOV. Oh yes. I do.

*(*BOBCHINSKY*'s head pops in at the door.)*

GOVERNOR. Charitable institutions. The district school. Methods of instruction in the sciences.

HLESTAKOV. Oh! By all means!

GOVERNOR. The police stations. The jail. You should know how we handle the criminal classes.

HLESTAKOV. No, no, I think we can skip all *that*. I *much* prefer charitable institutions.

GOVERNOR. Now, will you come to our place in your carriage, or shall I bring you in my chaise?

HLESTAKOV. Oh! Well, your chaise would be most welcome.

GOVERNOR *(to* DOBCHINSKY*)*. There won't be room for you now.

DOBCHINSKY. That's all right.

GOVERNOR *(to* DOBCHINSKY, *secretly)*. Two notes. One to the Director of Charities. One to my wife. Run over with them now. (DOBCHINSKY *nods. To* HLESTAKOV:) Permit me, in your presence, to jot down a line to my wife—telling her of your imminent arrival.

HLESTAKOV. Whatever for? But why not? Here's ink. As for paper, how about this bill?

GOVERNOR. Fine. *(While writing he talks to himself:)* We'll see how things go after lunch and a bottle of something strong. The local Madeira isn't all that good but it's strong enough to knock an elephant off its legs. I must find out what he's like and what I have to fear from him. *(He gives the notes to* DOBCHINSKY *who goes to the door which at this very moment comes off its hinges so that* BOBCHINSKY *comes flying into the room door in hand. Everyone gives a cry.* BOBCHINSKY *picks himself up.)*

HLESTAKOV. Well! I do hope you're not hurt?

BOBCHINSKY. No, no, nothing worth mentioning, just a bump on the nose. I'll run over to the Doctor's, he'll put plaster on it.

GOVERNOR *(making a sign of reproach to* BOBCHINSKY *but talking to* HLESTAKOV*)*. It's really nothing. Shall we go? Your servant can bring your luggage. *(*OSSIP *nods.* GOVERNOR *shows* HLESTAKOV *out, turning in the doorway to say to* BOBCHINSKY:) Couldn't you find someplace else for your tumbling act?

ACT THREE

Same as Act One. The GOVERNOR'S WIFE *and his daughter* MARYA *are still at the window.*

GOVERNOR'S WIFE. We've been at this window a whole hour now. Your primping! *(To herself:)* She was ready but she must go on primping! I should've paid no attention. And now, as if to spite us, not a soul in sight! It's a ghost town.

MARYA. We may know more any minute. Avdotya will be back. *(She looks out of the window and shrieks.)* Mamma! Someone's coming!

GOVERNOR'S WIFE. Where? You imagine things. But there *is* someone. Who? Short. A gentleman. Who can it be?

MARYA. Dobchinsky.

GOVERNOR'S WIFE. You do imagine things, that's not Dobchinsky. *(She waves to whoever it is.)*

MARYA. It *is* Dobchinsky.

GOVERNOR'S WIFE. Don't contradict.

MARYA. Look again. It's Dobchinsky.

GOVERNOR'S WIFE. Of course, it's Dobchinsky. Why are you always arguing? *(Shouting through the window:)* Hurry up! No, tell me now, from the street! Tell me!! *(Moving a little away from the window, annoyed.)* He won't speak till he gets indoors, the imbecile. *(Enter* DOBCHINSKY.*)* I thought you were the one man I could trust. But when the others run off, you run off. And I agreed to be godmother to both your daughters! Aren't you ashamed?

DOBCHINSKY. But, dear lady, to show my respect for you, I've run all the way from the inn. How are you, Marya?

MARYA. Good morning, Pyotr Ivanovitch.

GOVERNOR'S WIFE. Well, what happened at the inn? Tell us!

DOBCHINSKY. Your husband has sent you this note.

GOVERNOR'S WIFE. What sort of man is he, a general?

DOBCHINSKY. As good as a general. Such culture! Such manners!

GOVERNOR'S WIFE. Then he *is* the man they wrote my husband about.

DOBCHINSKY. The very one. I was the first to discover it. Pyotr Ivanovitch and I.

GOVERNOR'S WIFE. Well, tell us, tell us.

DOBCHINSKY. Everything went well in the end but at first he gave your husband a pretty cool reception. He was mad as hell and said everything at the inn was all wrong but he wouldn't come stay with him and didn't want to see the jail. He changed when he found your husband hadn't done anything wrong, and they've gone to inspect the hospital. At first your husband thought there must have been a secret report against him. *I* was scared, too.

GOVERNOR'S WIFE. But *you've* nothing to be afraid of, you're not in Government Service.

DOBCHINSKY. A person can't help getting the wind up when an Illustrious Personage is speaking.

GOVERNOR'S WIFE. Nonsense. But what's he like, old or young?

DOBCHINSKY. Young. About twenty-three. But very mature. "I am ready to go, if you wish it, I am ready to go there." "I am so fond of reading and writing. Tiresome that it's dark in this room."

GOVERNOR'S WIFE. Black hair or blond?

DOBCHINSKY. Auburn. Eyes quick as a squirrel's—they can make a man feel uncomfortable.

GOVERNOR'S WIFE *(reading the note)*. What's this your father says? "My position, my love, was truly excruciating, but, trusting in God's mercy, two dill pickles, and a half-portion of caviar, one ruble twenty-five kopecks . . ." What!?

DOBCHINSKY. It's written on an old bill.

GOVERNOR'S WIFE. I see. "Trusting in God's mercy, I believe all will be well. Please get a room ready for our illustrious guest, the one with the yellow wallpaper. Don't bother laying in food for supper: we are having a big lunch at the hospital. But tell Abdul to send you lots of his best wine or I'll vandalize his wine cellar. I remain, *chérie,* your Anton." Heavens, we must hurry. Mishka! *(Enter* MISHKA. *She speaks to him:)* Tell the coachman to drive over to Abdul's for wine. The best—or else. Then get the spare room ready for a visitor: bed, washstand, everything.

(Exit MISHKA.*)*

DOBCHINSKY. I'll go see how the inspection's going.

(He leaves.)

GOVERNOR'S WIFE. Now, Marya, we must decide what to wear. He's from Petersburg: everything must be *comme il faut.* For you, best would be the light blue dress with the flounces.

MARYA. But the Judge's daughter always wears blue. So does the Director of Charities' daughter. I'd better wear my flowered dress.

GOVERNOR'S WIFE. Anything to contradict me! The blue is better because I intend to wear straw yellow.

MARYA. It doesn't suit you.

GOVERNOR'S WIFE. Straw yellow doesn't suit me?

MARYA. No. You need dark eyes to go with straw yellow.

GOVERNOR'S WIFE. I *have* dark eyes. When I have my fortune told, they tell me I'm Queen of Clubs.

MARYA. You should be Queen of Hearts.

GOVERNOR'S WIFE. I have *never* been Queen of Hearts. *(Goes out with* MARYA *and speaks these lines from offstage:)* What will the girl think of next? Queen of Hearts indeed!

(A door opens. MISHKA *is sweeping dust through it. At another door,* OSSIP *enters with a suitcase on his head.)*

OSSIP. Which way?

MISHKA. This way, Dad!

OSSIP. Let me lay this down a minute. Things are much heavier on an empty stomach.

MISHKA. Will the General be here soon, daddykins?

OSSIP. What general?

MISHKA. Your master. Isn't he a General?

OSSIP. Oh, sure.

MISHKA. He's more than a General?

OSSIP. I guess so.

MISHKA. So, *that's* what the fuss is about.

OSSIP. If you're so smart, get me something to eat.

MISHKA. The food for *you* isn't ready yet. When your master sits down to eat, you'll get some of the same.

OSSIP. How about the food for *you?*

MISHKA. Cabbage soup, buckwheat, pies.

OSSIP. I'll take it. Help me with this suitcase. Over there?

(MISHKA *indicates the door it is to be taken through. Enter, through the main doors, the* COP *of Act One, then* HLESTAKOV, *the* GOVERNOR, *then the* DIRECTOR OF CHARITIES, *the* SUPER-INTENDENT OF SCHOOLS, DOBCHINSKY *and* BOBCHINSKY, *the latter with plaster on his nose. When the* GOVERNOR *notices a scrap of paper littering the floor, he signals to the* COP *to remove it and he does so.)*

HLESTAKOV. You have very fine institutions in your town, and you show a visitor everything. In other towns I was shown nothing.

GOVERNOR. In other towns, I might venture, the functionaries protect their own interests. Here we strive to please our superiors by exemplary conduct and eternal vigilance.

HLESTAKOV. The luncheon was good too. I think I ate too much. D'you lunch like that every day?

GOVERNOR. Just when entertaining guests.

HLESTAKOV. Gather ye rosebuds while ye may! I'm all for pleasure! What was that fish called?

DIRECTOR OF CHARITIES *(trotting up).* Labardán—it's salted scrod.

HLESTAKOV. Labardán. And where was it we lunched, at the hospital?

DIRECTOR OF CHARITIES. Just so. A charitable institution.

HLESTAKOV. Oh, I remember. Empty beds all over the place. Have the patients all recovered?

DIRECTOR OF CHARITIES. Twelve beds occupied. The others, yes, have all recovered. In many Russian hospitals, the inmates die like flies. Ours get well like flies. Arrive in hospital and instantly recover. That's what good management does for you.

GOVERNOR. How harrowing a Governor's work is! Everything is *his* business, cleanliness, repairs, reconstruction . . . How could it all go well? Yet, in this town, with God's help, it does. Many Russian governors feather their own nest, but you know what I say to myself in bed at night? "Almighty God, help me with one thing: to give satisfaction to my superiors!" Whether they reward me will be for them to decide, my heart is at peace. The streets swept, prison inmates cared for, very few drunks around, what more could one wish for? Rewards and honors are nice, but do I need them? They have their allure, but, for me, virtue has more.

DIRECTOR OF CHARITIES *(to himself)*. What a bullshit artist.

HLESTAKOV. Such thoughts occupy *my* mind, too, sometimes. I give expression to them in prose. Or even verse.

BOBCHINSKY *(to* DOBCHINSKY*)*. So well put! How he must've *studied!*

HLESTAKOV. How do you amuse yourselves around here? Anyone play cards?

GOVERNOR *(to himself)*. Oho, I see. *(To him:)* Heaven forbid, sir. I've hardly ever seen a pack of cards! An occasional glimpse of a King of Diamonds has made me feel a little sick. When I constructed a house of cards for my children one time, the damn things haunted my dreams for weeks.

SUPERINTENDENT OF SCHOOLS *(to himself)*. He played me last night and won a hundred rubles.

GOVERNOR. I prefer to devote all my time to my country!

HLESTAKOV. *All* your time? If a fellow thinks of his country just when he should double his stakes . . . Well, no, all I mean is: there's a time for play, too.

(Enter the GOVERNOR'S WIFE *and* MARYA.*)*

GOVERNOR. May I introduce my wife and daughter?

HLESTAKOV *(bowing)*. What a pleasure, madam, to see *you!*

GOVERNOR'S WIFE. An even greater pleasure to meet our distinguished visitor.

HLESTAKOV. No pleasure *could* be greater than mine.

GOVERNOR'S WIFE. Oh sir, your compliments! Won't you be seated?

HLESTAKOV. Is it not sufficient bliss to *stand* beside you, madam? But your wish being my command, I must sit, must I not? An even greater bliss!

GOVERNOR'S WIFE. Never would I command *you*, sir. But how boring you must find it—away from Petersburg.

HLESTAKOV. You have something there. When a man of the world, *vous comprenez,* finds himself in dirty inns amid rustic ignorance—*(He brings himself up short.)* Yet good fortune can change anything! *(He looks deep into her eyes.)*

GOVERNOR'S WIFE. I appreciate *how* boring you must find it.

HLESTAKOV. And I appreciate how good fortune can change it.

GOVERNOR'S WIFE. Now there's a compliment I don't deserve.

HLESTAKOV. Ah, madam, but you do.

GOVERNOR'S WIFE. Here I am, out in the country—

HLESTAKOV. Does not the country have its rolling landscape, its secret caverns? I don't say it's Petersburg. Petersburg is . . . life itself. You might think I was a copying clerk there, a mere pen pusher. Not so. I am on friendly terms with the head of my department, so friendly that he claps me on the shoulder and cries: "You must come to dinner with me, my boy!" I do look in at the office. Once a day. For two or three minutes. Just to tell'em what to do. And then that poor rat, the copying clerk, must scratch and scribble away. They offered me the job of Collegiate Assessor,* but I thought, "Why bother?" On the stairs outside the office, the porter runs after me with a shoe brush. "Allow me, Ivan Alexandrovitch," says he, "to clean your boots." *(To the other three men:)* But why remain standing, everyone? Please sit down. *(The three mutter proper little nothings.)* Rank, did you say? Never mind rank. *(They all sit.)* Rank indeed! I do my utmost to pass unnoticed. Why do I never succeed? Why is it, that whenever I pop up, voices call out: "There goes Ivan Alexandrovitch!" I was once mistaken for the Commander in Chief of all the Russias, and a veritable army of soldiers came flying out of the guardhouse, saluting!

GOVERNOR'S WIFE. Fancy that now!

HLESTAKOV. In the city, I'm friends with the prettiest actresses. Having written a few trifles for the stage, I move in literary circles. Very friendly with Pushkin. "Pushkin, old chap," I say,

---

*Eighth rank in the Service, whereas Hlestakov is in the fourteenth and lowest.

"how's it goin'?" "So-so, old chap," says he, "only so-so."
What a character, old Pushkin.

GOVERNOR'S WIFE. And *you* write! That must be frightfully thrilling. Do your things appear in the magazines?

HLESTAKOV. Some of them have: The Marriage of Figaro, Robert
the Devil, Norma, I don't remember them all. I had no intention
of writing plays at all but the Director of the Petersburg Theatres
said I absolutely had to. So I wrote a play in a single evening
much to the surprise of the town. A "ready wit" somebody
called me. You may have seen my stuff under other by-lines,
such as Baron Brambeus.

GOVERNOR'S WIFE. You are the famous Baron Brambeus?!

HLESTAKOV. I wrote The Frigate of Hope. I wrote The Moscow
Times.

GOVERNOR'S WIFE. Yuri Miloslavski* —is that yours?

HLESTAKOV. Definitely.

GOVERNOR'S WIFE. I thought so from the first.

MARYA. The name on the title page is Zagoskin.

GOVERNOR'S WIFE. Oh, you always argue!

HLESTAKOV. But she's right. There are two novels with that title.
I wrote the other one.

GOVERNOR'S WIFE. The one *I* read. It's fabulous.

HLESTAKOV *(shrugging)*. I live by my pen, after all. My home is
the first house of the whole city. Known to the *hoi polloi* as
"Ivan's Place." *(Talking to the whole gathering:)* And let me
hereby issue an open invitation to one and all to visit me there. I
give balls, by the way.

GOVERNOR'S WIFE. I can just imagine the *grandeur*, the *good taste*
of those balls.

HLESTAKOV. The keynote is simplicity. On the table, a water
melon that cost seven hundred rubles. The soup comes by boat

---

*Baron Brambeus was the pen name of a popular writer at the time. *The Frigate
of Hope* was a popular novel. *Yuri Miloslavski* was a well-known story. The
Moscow Times is the adaptor's perhaps sly rendering of what would more
literally be The Moscow Telegraph: Hlestakov writes whole journals just as he
brings out whole operas as magazine articles!

from Paris . . . I attend balls nightly. Then there is the whist club: the Russian Foreign Minister, the French Ambassador, the German Ambassador, and me. We wear ourselves out at whist. When I get home, I hardly have the strength to climb the four flights of stairs and tell the cook, "Take my overcoat, Mavrushka, take my overcoat!" But I'm forgetting: I live on the first floor. The staircase cost me a mint. In my antechamber, you can hear the Counts and Princes humming like so many bees, BUZZ BUZZ BUZZ. There was a *Minister* once—*(The* GOVERNOR *and the others are alarmed at the word Minister.)* In their letters these people address me as Your Excellency. I took charge of a whole Department once. The Director had gone off somewhere, and people were asking who would take his place. Generals wanted the job, but it was too hard for them. So my name came up. Suddenly the streets were full of couriers: can you imagine 35,000 couriers in one street? "Come direct the Department!" I went out on the landing in my dressing gown and was going to refuse but then I thought: "it might come to the ears of the Tsar." So, "Very well," I reluctantly say, "I'll do it but watch out." And they sure had to watch out because I tore right through the Department like a tornado. They shook like aspen leaves. *(The* GOVERNOR *and his colleagues shake like aspen leaves.* HLESTAKOV *is emboldened thereby.)* I put the fear of God into them! Gave the Imperial Council hell! "I know my POWER," I told 'em, "I'm in and out of the Royal Palace! I am EVERYWHERE! Tomorrow I'll be a FIELD MARSHAL!"

(In the middle of the last word he slides off his chair onto the floor. The officials pick him up respectfully.)

GOVERNOR. Would Your Excellency care to lie down? Your room is ready.

HLESTAKOV. Nonsense. Fine. Lie down? You gave me such a lunch, I'm so happy, so happy! Labardán, Labardán! *(With a flourish on this word, he retires to his room, followed by the* GOVERNOR.*)*

BOBCHINSKY *(to* DOBCHINSKY*).* Now I know what it means to be a MAN. I almost died of fright. What can his rank be, Pyotr Ivanovitch?

DOBCHINSKY. General.

BOBCHINSKY. Generalissimo. He gives the Imperial Council hell. Let's go and tell the Judge. Goodbye, Ma'am.

(They leave.)

DIRECTOR OF CHARITIES *(to the* SUPERINTENDENT OF SCHOOLS*).* I'm scared too. I couldn't say what of. We're not even in uniform. But when he sobers up, he may send a report to Petersburg.

(He leaves, plunged in thought, with the SUPERINTENDENT OF SCHOOLS, *both saying "Goodbye, Ma'am" at the door.)*

GOVERNOR'S WIFE. What a charming young man!

MARYA. He's cute.

GOVERNOR'S WIFE. A real man of fashion. What manners! Puts me in quite a flutter when he keeps looking at me.

MARYA. Actually, he was looking at me.

GOVERNOR'S WIFE. Don't be perverse.

MARYA. Only he *was*.

GOVERNOR'S WIFE. Forever arguing. Forever contradicting. Why would he look at you?

MARYA. He did, that's all. He gave me a look when he brought up literature, and when he spoke of playing whist with the ambassadors he gave me another look.

GOVERNOR'S WIFE. A look. A passing glance. That's nothing.

GOVERNOR *(entering on tiptoe)*. Sh-sh!

GOVERNOR'S WIFE. What is it?

GOVERNOR. I'm sorry I got him so drunk, what if only half of what he said is true? *(Pause.) In vino veritas!* What's in the heart is on the tongue! It was *all* true. Oh, I expect he embroidered a bit here and there, but he does play whist with ambassadors! He's in and out of the Royal Palace all the time! Phew! I feel I'm on the brink of a precipice. Or just about to be hanged.

GOVERNOR'S WIFE. For rank I care not a jot. I see in him, quite simply, a MAN—of course of great culture and accustomed to the very best society.

GOVERNOR *(to himself)*. Women! So damn trivial. And you never know what they'll blurt out. Then they go unpunished, and it's the husband that takes the fall. *(To her:)* My love, you made free with him as if he'd been Dobchinsky.

GOVERNOR'S WIFE. Think nothing of it, husband, though, then again, we two *(indicating her daughter)* know what we know.

GOVERNOR *(to himself)*. No use talking to women but I'm so upset. *(He opens the door and speaks in the doorway:)* Mishka, get me that cop. *(Pause.)* Strange times we live in. We used to expect distinguished gentlemen to *look* distinguished. But this little whipper snapper, who would ever guess? He's not in uniform. A man in uniform looks distinguished while a man in a swallow-tail coat looks like a fly with its wings cut off ... This morning at the inn he kept up appearances. I thought we'd never get anything *real* out of him. But at lunch the wine worked. He said too much, that's all. Must be because he's young and hasn't been at it long ...

(Enter OSSIP. They run towards him, beckoning.)

GOVERNOR'S WIFE. Come right in, my man.

GOVERNOR. Sh-sh! *(In a whisper:)* Is he asleep yet?

OSSIP. Just yawning and stretching, sir.

GOVERNOR'S WIFE. What's your name?

OSSIP. Ossip, ma'am.

GOVERNOR *(to the women)*. Leave him to me. *(To OSSIP:)* Well, my friend, did they feed you well?

OSSIP. Very well, sir.

GOVERNOR'S WIFE. Do many Counts—and Princes!—come to see your master?

OSSIP *(to himself)*. How shall I handle this? They've fed me well, maybe they'll feed me better. *(To them:)* Quite a few Counts, yes, ma'am.

MARYA. I think your master's gorgeous.

GOVERNOR'S WIFE. Tell us, would you, just how he—

GOVERNOR. Oh, cut it out. Now tell me, my good man—

GOVERNOR'S WIFE. What your master's rank is.

OSSIP. Oh, the usual.

GOVERNOR. Don't ask such dumb questions. *(To OSSIP:)* Now, my man, describe your master to us. Is he very strict? Finds fault a lot?

OSSIP *(cautiously)*. Well, he does like things done right. Yeah. Everything has to be just so.

GOVERNOR. You have a good face, my friend. You're a good *man*. Tell me this—

GOVERNOR'S WIFE. Does your master wear a uniform at home?

GOVERNOR. Quiet, females. This is a matter of life and death. *(To* OSSIP:*)* My friend, I like you. An extra glass of tea might not come amiss. In this cold weather and you so far from home. Here's a couple of rubles for some tea.

OSSIP *(taking the money)*. Thanks for helping a poor man out, sir.

GOVERNOR. Pleased to do what I can. Tell me this—

GOVERNOR'S WIFE. What sort of eyes does your master like, green, blue, light, dark?

MARYA. I adore his nose.

GOVERNOR. Quiet, I said. *(To* OSSIP:*)* What are the things your master takes note of? What, for instance, does he like best when travelling?

OSSIP. Oh, I don't know. Maybe just being . . . well entertained.

GOVERNOR. Well entertained?

OSSIP. And seeing that *I'm* well entertained. "Ossip," he'll say, "were you well entertained here?" "No," I say sometimes, "I was not." "That's bad," he replies, "remind me of this when we get back home."

GOVERNOR. I did give you money for tea. Here's some for buns.

OSSIP. You're kindness itself, sir.

GOVERNOR'S WIFE. Come and talk with *me*, Ossip. *I'll* give you something too.

MARYA. Take your master a big kiss from me.

(HLESTAKOV *is heard coughing in the next room.*)

GOVERNOR. Sh-sh! *(He walks on tiptoe again. The rest of the conversation is in a whisper.)* Run along, you two, you've done enough talking.

GOVERNOR'S WIFE. Let's be going, Marya. There's something about our guest that I can only tell you in private.

GOVERNOR *(to himself)*. At it again, the females. Their tittle tattle makes a man wish he was deaf. *(To* OSSIP:*)* Now my friend—

(Enter the COP.*)* Those boots of yours! Talk about a ton of bricks! Where have you been anyway?

COP *(loudly).* Acting on instructions, I—

GOVERNOR. Sh-sh! *(Stops his mouth.)* Phew! *(To* OSSIP*:)* Take care of your master and remember—all that we have is yours.

(Exit OSSIP.*)* Now, you, stand at the front door. No outsiders to be let in, understand? If anyone has a petition—if anyone looks like he *might* have a petition—*against* me, *to* me, whatever —throw him out by the scruff of his neck! Kick him on the shins! *(He gives a demonstration.)* Got it? Sh-sh! *(He follows the* COP *out on tiptoe.)*

HLESTAKOV. Pleased to meet you. Sit down and have a cigar.

SUPERINTENDENT OF SCHOOLS *(uncertainly, to himself:)* Should I or shouldn't I?

HLESTAKOV. They're not bad cigars, take one, oh it may not be what you'd get in Petersburg for twenty-five rubles: *my* type cigar. Here.

(SUPERINTENDENT OF SCHOOLS, having taken a cigar, is now being given a candle to light it with. He tries to light the wrong end of the cigar, then in panic drops the cigar on the floor.)

SUPERINTENDENT OF SCHOOLS *(to himself, very disgusted).* My timidity has ruined everything.

HLESTAKOV. You don't like cigars, do you? They're one of my little weaknesses. Women are another. How about you? What's your preference, blonde or brunette? *(SUPERINTENDENT OF SCHOOLS is tongue-tied.)* Blonde or brunette?

SUPERINTENDENT OF SCHOOLS. Well, um, *I'm* not worthy . . . to have an opinion . . .

HLESTAKOV. You're blushing.

SUPERINTENDENT OF SCHOOLS. I'm, um, over-awed by . . . Your Excellency.

HLESTAKOV. I *am* awe-inspiring, aren't I? I've been learning that. Women can't hold out against me, can they?

SUPERINTENDENT OF SCHOOLS. I'm sure they can't.

HLESTAKOV. Another thing. I was cleaned out on the way here. Can you lend me three hundred?

SUPERINTENDENT OF SCHOOLS *(to himself).* What will happen if I don't have it on me? *(Searches his pockets.)* I do, I'm saved. *(Hands* HLESTAKOV *the money.)*

HLESTAKOV. Hey, thanks.

SUPERINTENDENT OF SCHOOLS *(standing to attention, hand on sword).* And now I will trouble you no longer with my humble presence.

HLESTAKOV. Bye.

SUPERINTENDENT OF SCHOOLS *(scurrying out, to himself).* Maybe he won't even glance at the schoolroom.

(Enter the DIRECTOR OF CHARITIES, *stands to attention, hand on sword.)*

DIRECTOR OF CHARITIES. I have the honor to introduce myself: Zemlyanika, Court Councillor, Director of Charities.

HLESTAKOV. How are you? Pray be seated.

DIRECTOR OF CHARITIES. I have already had the honor of receiving you at the hospital.

HLESTAKOV. That's right. That luncheon!

DIRECTOR OF CHARITIES. We do our best for Mother Russia.

HLESTAKOV. Food and drink are also among my weaknesses. Look: you weren't as tall yesterday, were you? As tall as you are now?

DIRECTOR OF CHARITIES. Wasn't I? *(He is thrown.)* In the performance of my duties, I might almost be called a fanatic. *(Draws his chair closer to* HLESTAKOV's, *and lowers his voice.)* The Postmaster never does a thing, that's why the postal service down here is in such disarray. You might want to look into it. The Judge does nothing either—except hunt rabbits and hares. Did you see all those dogs in his courtroom? He's a relative of mine, and a *very* close friend, but in honesty I must tell you he's a bad character in all respects. You noticed the landowner Dobchinsky? Well, he only has to leave his home, and the Judge is there with his wife. Dobchinsky's wife. Have you seen the Dobchinsky children? Not one of them resembles Dobchinsky. They're the spitting image of the Judge.

HLESTAKOV. Well, who'd have guessed all this?

DIRECTOR OF CHARITIES. And the School Superintendent. Why was he ever entrusted with *that* job? He's a veritable *Jacobin.* Oh yes. Instilling those subversive ideas in the Russian young. I'll put that in writing if you want.

HLESTAKOV. Oh please do, I like to have something exciting to read. What's your name again?

DIRECTOR OF CHARITIES. Zemlyanika.

HLESTAKOV. Any children?

DIRECTOR OF CHARITIES. Five. Two of' em grown up now.

HLESTAKOV. And their names?

DIRECTOR OF CHARITIES. Nikolai, Ivan, Yelisaveta, Marya, and Perepetuya.

HLESTAKOV. Tremendous.

DIRECTOR OF CHARITIES. Now I must not trouble you any further with my humble presence, thus robbing you of time dedicated to duty . . .

HLESTAKOV *(accompanying him to the door)*. Come again, and give me more of that . . . inside dope . . . I love it . . . *(DIRECTOR OF CHARITIES has now left the room. HLESTAKOV calls him back.)* Come back a minute, what was your name again?

DIRECTOR OF CHARITIES *(back)*. Zemlyanika.

HLESTAKOV. Right. Well, I was completely cleaned out on the way here. Can you lend me four hundred rubles?

DIRECTOR OF CHARITIES. Oh, yes.

HLESTAKOV. Hey, I'm in luck. Thanks.

(DIRECTOR OF CHARITIES gives him the money and leaves. Enter BOBCHINSKY and DOBCHINSKY.)

BOBCHINSKY. I have the honor to introduce myself: Pyotr Ivanovitch Bobchinsky, Resident.

DOBCHINSKY. Pyotr Ivanovitch Dobchinsky, Landowner.

HLESTAKOV. Oh yes, I remember *you* from yesterday. You fell in, door in hand. How's your nose?

BOBCHINSKY. Fine. See? All healed up.

HLESTAKOV. Great. D'you have any money on you?

DOBCHINSKY. Money? Why?

HLESTAKOV. I need a thousand rubles.

BOBCHINSKY. Oh dear. A thousand? *(To DOBCHINSKY:)* What about you?

DOBCHINSKY. My money is all tied up at the bank.

HLESTAKOV. How about a hundred?

BOBCHINSKY *(fumbling in his pockets)*. Do you have it? I only have forty.

DOBCHINSKY *(looking in his wallet)*. I only have twenty-five.

BOBCHINSKY. Look in that lining. There's a hole in your righthand pocket. There may be some cash in the lining.

DOBCHINSKY. There isn't.

HLESTAKOV. Oh well, I just thought I'd ask. Sixty-five is quite all right. *(They hand it to him.)* Thanks.

DOBCHINSKY. And now I make bold to ask your assistance in a matter of some delicacy.

HLESTAKOV. Ha?

DOBCHINSKY. My eldest son, you see, was born out of wedlock. Of course, we then married, so everything is right and proper. But now I want him to get my name: Dobchinsky.

HLESTAKOV. Dobchinsky he shall be.

DOBCHINSKY. He's so talented, that's why. Recites all manner of poetry. Does all sorts of carpentry with nothing but a small knife . . . Am I right, Bobchinsky?

BOBCHINSKY. Right, Dobchinsky.

HLESTAKOV. I shall mention it in the right quarter. *(Turning to* BOBCHINSKY:*)* And what do *you* have on your mind?

BOBCHINSKY. When you're back in Petersburg, with all those Senators and Admirals, ask them did they know that, in such a town, there lives a man called Pyotr Ivanovitch Bobchinsky.

HLESTAKOV. That all?

BOBCHINSKY. Well, if you do have a chance to talk to the Tsar, would you mind saying: "Imperial Majesty, did you know that, in such a town, there lives a man called Pyotr Ivanovitch Bobchinsky?"

HLESTAKOV. I'll do that.

DOBCHINSKY. Excuse us for troubling you with our presence.

BOBCHINSKY. Excuse us for troubling you with our presence.

HLESTAKOV. My pleasure. *(Having seen them out, to himself:)* It would seem that all these people take me for a government official of some importance. When I was so drunk yesterday, I must have told them quite a tale. What clowns! I must tell my friend Tryapitchkin about this. Being a professional writer who wields a wicked pen and has the ear of Petersburg he can make a pot of money off a story like this. What matter if he adds to it and exaggerates a bit? Ossip! Ink and paper! *(In the doorway,* OSSIP *says:* "Just a minute!") Good guys, these, lending me . . . how much is it? Three hundred from the Judge, three hundred from the Postmaster, six, seven, eight . . . Ugh, what a filthy bill . . . nine, over one thousand rubles . . . So where's that infantry captain who beat me at cards! *Now* I'm ready for him! *(Re-enter* OSSIP *with ink and paper. As he starts to write a letter:)* You see how it is, dumb bell? I'm really appreciated around here.

OSSIP. That's good, but you know what?

HLESTAKOV. What?

OSSIP. It's time for a change.

HLESTAKOV. We should leave? Now?

OSSIP. Count your blessings. You've had two good days. Don't tempt fate. There are some very fast horses on hand.

HLESTAKOV *(pouting as he writes).* Tomorrow then!

OSSIP. Today! They've taken you for someone else.' Besides, your father will say: "The little wretch has been *dawdling* again!" Think of those fast horses.

HLESTAKOV *(writing).* Very well. But let's get this letter in the post first. You can get me my travel pass at the same time. About the horses, make sure we get the very best. And pay the drivers to treat me as a Special Messenger, driving like lightning, singing as they drive! *(Writing.)* Tryapitchkin will split his sides laughing!

OSSIP. The man here will mail the letter, I'd better pack.

HLESTAKOV. Good. Just bring me a candle.

OSSIP *(offstage).* Stand ready to take a letter to the post office. Official business, no stamp needed. Then have the horses sent over. The best they have. No fare to pay: the Crown will pay. And be quick.

HLESTAKOV *(writing).* I wonder where his pad is now? Since he never pays the rent, he keeps on the move. I'll take a chance on that *Post Office Street* address . . .

(He writes an address on the envelope. OSSIP *comes back in with a candle.* HLESTAKOV *seals the letter. Voice of the* COP *is heard:* Hey, you, Mr. Bushy Beard, stop shoving! No one admitted!!" OSSIP *takes the letter from* HLESTAKOV *out of the room. Shopkeepers' Voices are heard from offstage:* "Let us in, let us in, we're here on business!" *etcetera. The uproar grows at this interchange between police and crowd.)*

HLESTAKOV. What's all the noise about?

OSSIP *(who is back, looking out through a window)*. Some shop-keepers are trying to get in, but the cop won't admit them. I get it: they wanna see *you*, they're waving petitions.

HLESTAKOV *(at the window in a flash, raising a hand for silence)*. Now, what is it, my good friends?

A SHOPKEEPER'S VOICE. Petitions, sir!

ANOTHER. Let us in, Your Excellency, we are men of property!

HLESTAKOV. That's right. Ossip, go down and tell that guy to let 'em in. *(To someone outside:)* Let's have that petition! *(He is given a petition from outside. Reading it:)* "To the Honorable Excellency and Master of Finance"—there is no such title, of course—"from Abdul, Merchant." *(Enter the Shopkeepers, led by the aforementioned ABDUL. They bring sugar-loaves and a basket of wine.)* Well, hello, my friends, what can I do for you? *(Various answers are called out to the effect of "Save us from total ruin!")* Save you from total ruin, eh? Sounds like a good idea. Where's Mr. Abdul, Merchant?

ABDUL. That's me, your Excellency.

HLESTAKOV. So you be the spokesman.

ABDUL. Well, it's this Governor, sir. He's ruining us. Billeting soldiers on us, persecuting us in every way.

ANOTHER SHOPKEEPER *(interrupting)*. Last week he pulled me by the beard and yelled: "Tartar!"

ABDUL *(continuing)*. And we've done right by him. We've given him presents. Dresses for his wife and daughter. But he acts like he owns us. Walks in our shops and grabs anything he wants, or even orders it sent over—we have to send it or else.

HLESTAKOV. He's a regular son of a bitch, ha?

ABDUL. Well, yes, sir.

ANOTHER SHOPKEEPER *(interrupting)*. When I see him coming, I hide *everything*. He doesn't just steal dainties but anything at all —plums my workers wouldn't touch, they're so old and moldy —he'll stick a handful of 'em in his pocket.

ABDUL *(continuing)*. On his Name Day we take him all sorts of goodies. Then he claims he has two Name Days. And we have to deliver.

HLESTAKOV. He should have been a highway robber.

ABDUL *(nodding)*. But, refuse him, and he'll quarter a regiment on you. Object to that, and he'll padlock your store.

HLESTAKOV. Resorts to torture, does he?

ABDUL *(nodding)*. Putting you on a diet of red herring with nothing to drink. You get an unbearable thirst. "Of course," says he, "I wouldn't flog you, I wouldn't use torture, those things are against the law but . . ."

HLESTAKOV. You know, I think he should be sent to Siberia.

ABDUL. As long as he's nowhere near this town.

ANOTHER SHOPKEEPER. Meanwhile, Excellency, please accept these sugar-loaves and this wine.

HLESTAKOV. That would be bribery! I just couldn't! What I need is a loan. Who can loan me three hundred rubles?

(The Shopkeepers put their heads together.)

ABDUL *(after this brief conference)*. Five hundred. If you'll help us.

HLESTAKOV. All right. I've nothing against an honest loan.

ABDUL *(offering him the five hundred on a silver tray)*. And please accept the silver tray with it.

HLESTAKOV. I can always use a tray.

ABDUL. We'll leave the loaves and wine here for you to dispose of as you think fit.

ANOTHER SHOPKEEPER. Also some good stout string made in my workshops. It'll come in useful on your journeys.

ABDUL. Remember: our case is desperate.

(They leave. And now a woman's voice is heard from outside: "I have to see him, I have to see him!"*)*

HLESTAKOV. Now who's this? *(He is at the window now.)* What is it, my good woman?

WOMAN'S VOICE. There are two of us.

ANOTHER WOMAN'S VOICE. We both need your help.

HLESTAKOV. Let them in.

(Two women are admitted: the LOCKSMITH'S WIFE *and the* SERGEANT'S WIDOW.*)*

LOCKSMITH'S WIFE *(on her knees before* HLESTAKOV*)*. Help!

SERGEANT'S WIDOW (*on her knees before* HLESTAKOV). Help, Gracious Sir!

HLESTAKOV. But who are you?

SERGEANT'S WIDOW. The Sergeant's Widow.

LOCKSMITH'S WIFE. The Locksmith's Wife.

HLESTAKOV. And what do you want? One at a time now!

LOCKSMITH'S WIFE. Protection from the Governor, God curse him!

HLESTAKOV. What has he done this time?

LOCKSMITH'S WIFE. Sent my husband into the army when it wasn't his turn. And him being married, it's against the law.

HLESTAKOV. Whose turn was it?

LOCKSMITH'S WIFE. The tailor's son, you know that drunk. But his parents gave the Governor a present. Next in line was the draper's son but his mother gave the Governor's wife three bolts of linen. So he came to me. "What do you want with that husband? He's no good." "If he's no good," I reply, "that's no business of yours." "He's a thief," says he. "He never stole a thing in his life," say I. "His life ain't over yet," says he, "he'd be drafted next year anyway." So he took my husband, God curse him, God—

HLESTAKOV. All right. (*He waves her out.*) How about you?

LOCKSMITH'S WIFE (*on the way out*). Mercy, great sir! And don't forget!

SERGEANT'S WIDOW. He flogged me.

HLESTAKOV. How come?

SERGEANT'S WIDOW. By mistake, sir. After a fight among the women. The cops arrived late and picked on me. After the drubbing they gave me I couldn't sit down for two days.

HLESTAKOV. I can't un-flog you.

SERGEANT'S WIDOW. Make the Governor pay damages: they're *his* cops. And I can use the money.

HLESTAKOV. Couldn't we all? I'll see what I can do. (*He waves her out. Hands holding petitions are thrust in at the window.*) Who is it now? (*He goes to the window.*) That's all I need: Ossip, send them away, send them all away, I'm sick of this!

OSSIP *(shouting at the window).* Silence! *(He gets silence.)* Session over! Now go home! Come back tomorrow!

(The double doors open. Framed in the doorway, with other figures more dimly seen behind him, is the single figure of a man in a shaggy old overcoat, chin unshaven, lip swollen, a bandage around his face. Taking him in, OSSIP *strides straight to him and pushes him back through the doorway—both fists in his stomach. The doors slam. Enter* MARYA *from a side door.)*

MARYA *(a cry of fright).* Oh!

HLESTAKOV. Hello. What are you frightened of?

MARYA. I'm not frightened.

HLESTAKOV *(striking an attitude).* I'm flattered to be the kind of man you—but let me just ask this: where were you going?

MARYA. Nowhere.

HLESTAKOV. Let me ask this: *why* were you going nowhere?

MARYA. I thought maybe Mamma was here.

HLESTAKOV. *That* was why you were going nowhere?

MARYA. But I'm interrupting important business.

HLESTAKOV *(again striking an attitude).* What business more important than a single glance from eyes like those?

MARYA. I like the way you talk.

HLESTAKOV. May I enjoy the happiness of offering you a seat? You, of course, should have a THRONE, not a chair.

MARYA. Well, really, you know, I should be going. *(She sits.)*

HLESTAKOV. What a lovely kerchief.

MARYA. You're making fun of me. I know I'm very provincial.

HLESTAKOV. Would that *I* were that little kerchief embracing that lily white neck!

MARYA. I don't what you mean, sir. My kerchief? Hm. Funny weather today!

HLESTAKOV. Your lips, *mademoiselle*, rise above any kind of weather you might name!

MARYA. You say such things. Would you write some poetry in my album? I bet you know a lot of poetry.

HLESTAKOV. For your sake—anything. What poetry?

MARYA. Oh, you know, something different—new—

HLESTAKOV. Well, now, how's this? "Man is born to trouble—as the sparks—as the sparks what? yes: fly upward!" I could go on but, instead, do you know what I want to do? Offer you my love. It's those eyes—*(He moves his chair nearer hers.)*

MARYA. What is love? I have never known it. *(Moves her chair away.)*

HLESTAKOV. You're moving your chair away! Kindred souls should draw closer. And closer. *(He moves in.)*

MARYA *(moving away).* Distance, they say, can lend enchantment.

HLESTAKOV *(moving in).* Something else lends even more enchantment.

MARYA *(moving away).* I wonder what that something else could be?

HLESTAKOV. You could *imagine* we were miles apart though in fact we were in each others'—*(When he tries to pounce, she slips away to the window.)* How happy I should be, *mademoiselle,* to hold you in my arms.

MARYA *(intent on the sky outside).* What kind of bird is that? A magpie?

HLESTAKOV *(hastening over, and kissing her on the shoulder).* A magpie, yes.

MARYA *(reacting to the kiss).* Ha! You are too forward, my dear sir!

HLESTAKOV *(holding on to her).* Can you forgive me, do you think? Ever? For the cause was—love. Real live love!

MARYA. Pah! You think I'm some peasant girl you can just—

HLESTAKOV *(still holding on to her).* Love was the word. Besides, Marya dear, I meant no harm. Just innocent fun. Laugh it off. Laugh! *(He laughs.)* I am ready, in any case, to beg your forgiveness on my very knees. *(He falls on his knees.)* See? Now: forgive me!

(Enter the GOVERNOR'S WIFE. *She sees all.)*

GOVERNOR'S WIFE. Oh!

HLESTAKOV *(rising hastily).* Dear me.

GOVERNOR'S WIFE *(to her daughter).* May I ask what this means?

MARYA. Well, mamma, I, um—

GOVERNOR'S WIFE. Leave the room this minute. *(Marya does so, in tears.)* Excuse me, sir, but I am more than a little surprised—

HLESTAKOV *(to himself).* She's pretty sexy herself. *(Again falls to his knees:)* I love you. I'm dying for love of you.

GOVERNOR'S WIFE. On your knees—*again?* This floor is anything but clean.

HLESTAKOV. On my knees, I await the verdict: life or—death.

GOVERNOR'S WIFE. I don't think I follow you, sir. You are telling me your feelings for my daughter?

HLESTAKOV. I am telling you my feelings for *you*. Love. If you don't return my love, I am a dead man.

GOVERNOR'S WIFE. What?

HLESTAKOV. I am asking for your hand.

GOVERNOR'S WIFE. But, sir, I am already, in a certain sense, married.

HLESTAKOV. It's illegal then? Never mind. The poet has said it better than I can: "To happy valleys, purling streams, let's fly away!" I ask your hand in marriage!

(He is still on his knees when MARYA *comes back in.)*

MARYA *(talking as she enters).* Mamma, papa says—*(Then she sees all.)* Oh!

GOVERNOR'S WIFE. What do *you* want? Running around like a scalded cat. What's so surprising? How old are you—three? Eighteen: but when will she learn?

MARYA *(in tears).* But, mamma, I didn't know—

GOVERNOR'S WIFE. You're as fluttery as the Lyapkin-Tyapkin girls. Why model yourself on them? A girl's model should be her own mamma.

HLESTAKOV *(grabs* MARYA*'s hand, but speaks to* GOVERNOR'S WIFE*). Madame!* Please! Do not oppose our happiness! We ask your blessing on our everlasting love!

GOVERNOR'S WIFE *(amazed).* You mean—!?

HLESTAKOV. The verdict is life or—death.

GOVERNOR'S WIFE *(realizing, to her daughter).* So you see, you silly girl: for a worthless child like you, our illustrious guest went down on his knees! So what do you mean by running in here and getting mad at him? It would serve you right if I refused my consent. You don't deserve such bliss.

MARYA. I won't do it again, mamma, I won't do it again.

(Enter the GOVERNOR, *breathless.)*

GOVERNOR. You wouldn't ruin me, Your Excellency? You wouldn't ruin me, would you?

HLESTAKOV. I don't think so, why?

GOVERNOR. I know what they've been telling you, those shop-keepers, but I can report, on my honor, that not even half what they've told you is true. They short-change the whole town, they give short measure on all their scales. When that sergeant's widow said I flogged her, she was lying. She must have flogged herself.

HLESTAKOV. Oh, drat the sergeant's widow. I have other worries.

GOVERNOR. Don't believe them! They're all liars! The whole town knows that! Swindlers and—

GOVERNOR'S WIFE. Stop a minute. Ivan Alexandrovitch is doing us a very great honor: he's asking for our daughter's hand.

GOVERNOR. You off your rocker now? It never rains but it pours. Don't get mad, Excellency, she never was very strong in the head—

HLESTAKOV. But it's true, what she says. Madly in love with your daughter, I'm asking for—

GOVERNOR. I don't believe it!

GOVERNOR'S WIFE. But when he says so himself?

HLESTAKOV. I'm head over heels in love with your daughter!

GOVERNOR. I *daren't* believe it.

HLESTAKOV. And, if you don't give your consent, God knows what I may do to myself!

GOVERNOR. I still don't believe it.

GOVERNOR'S WIFE. Can't believe him when he tells you himself, lunkhead?

GOVERNOR. Even then!

HLESTAKOV. Well, consent, give your consent. I'm a desperate man. If I shoot myself, you will have to answer for it.

GOVERNOR. Oh my God, please don't be angry. Do what your Excellency thinks best. My head is swimming . . . It's not my fault!

GOVERNOR'S WIFE. At least give them your blessing.

(HLESTAKOV approaches the GOVERNOR with MARYA.)

GOVERNOR. May God bless you both! It's just not my fault!! *(HLESTAKOV kisses MARYA. The GOVERNOR stares.)* Good God, it's true, they're kissing! *(He rubs his eyes.)* Saints above, they're engaged to be married. *(He skips about the room and cries out for joy.)* Hooray for the Governor! Things have taken a new turn! Hooray for the Governor! Hooray!

(Enter OSSIP.)

OSSIP *(to HLESTAKOV).* The horses are ready, sir.

HLESTAKOV. Good. I'll be right with you.

GOVERNOR. What's this? Your Excellency isn't leaving?

HLESTAKOV. He is.

GOVERNOR. Then—what the—I thought . . . your Excellency had just deigned to hint at, um, wedding bells?

HLESTAKOV. That's right. This is a little side trip. To see my old uncle. He's rich, you know. I'll be back tomorrow.

GOVERNOR. I see. Then we must not presume to hold you a moment longer.

HLESTAKOV. *Au revoir,* my love. How can I express the depths of what I feel? Bye. *(He kisses MARYA's hand.)*

GOVERNOR. Need anything for the journey? You were short on cash, as I recall.

HLESTAKOV. Oh? *(Pause.)* Oh yes, that's right.

GOVERNOR. How much?

HLESTAKOV. Could you let me have another two—that is, four —hundred? Remember your little mistake? I never take advantage. Eight hundred in all?

GOVERNOR. Certainly. *(He takes four hundred from his wallet.)* I have brand-new bills!

HLESTAKOV. Brand-new bills bring luck. Thanks.

GOVERNOR. Yes, indeed.

HLESTAKOV. Much obliged for your hospitality. Never met with
such a warm reception in all my life. Goodbye, *Madame*. And
my darling *Mademoiselle*.

*(They all go out. The stage remains empty while we hear
offstage voices as follows:)*

HLESTAKOV. Goodbye, Marya, my angel!

GOVERNOR. You're using the public post carriage? It has no
springs!

HLESTAKOV. Springs make my head ache.

DRIVER. Whoa there, my beauties!

GOVERNOR. At least let me give you something for that wooden
seat. A rug?

HLESTAKOV. Oh, don't bother. But why not? Give us a rug.

GOVERNOR. Avdotya, that Persian rug with the blue pattern!

DRIVER. Whoa there!

GOVERNOR. And when shall we expect you back?

HLESTAKOV. Oh, tomorrow. Or the next day.

OSSIP. That the rug? Give it here!

DRIVER. Whoa there!

OSSIP. Now sit on it, *Excellency!*

HLESTAKOV. So goodbye, Mr. Governor!

GOVERNOR. Goodbye, Excellency!

BOTH WOMEN. Goodbye, Ivan!

HLESTAKOV. Goodbye, mamma.

DRIVER. Now, my beauties .... We're off!

(Jingle bells.)

ACT FIVE

The same as Acts One, Three, and Four. The GOVERNOR, *the* GOVERNOR'S WIFE, *and* MARYA.

GOVERNOR. Well? Never in your wildest dreams did you think a mere Governor's wife would become . . . *(He makes a large gesture.)*

GOVERNOR'S WIFE. *You* didn't. That's your *common* background. I always preferred . . . *respectable* people . . . I saw all this coming . . .

GOVERNOR. But *I'm* respectable, my dear! Oh, just think what fine birds we have become, what plumage, and perched at the top of the tree! As for those tattle tales, I'm gonna let them have it! Svistunov! *(Enter the* COP.*)* Bring me those shopkeepers. Make me a list of all those who came here with petitions, also those who wrote the petitions, and tell them what's happened, tell them what God in his infinite wisdom has decreed: THE GOVERNOR IS MARRYING HIS DAUGHTER TO SOMEONE WHO CAN DO ANYTHING. Shout it from the housetops! Ring the bells! Make a day of it! *(He waves the* COP *out.)* Where are we going to live now? Here?

GOVERNOR'S WIFE. In Petersburg. How could we live *here?*

GOVERNOR. Oh, it could be nice here. But then I won't be just a Governor any more, will I?

GOVERNOR'S WIFE. A Governor is less than the dust.

GOVERNOR. So what can I be? Popping in and out of the Royal Palace all the time, could he get me promoted to General? Or is that too much to hope?

GOVERNOR'S WIFE. Not too much at all.

GOVERNOR. A General! Decorations right across my chest! That red ribbon. That blue ribbon. Which do you prefer?

GOVERNOR'S WIFE. The blue ribbon.

GOVERNOR. And red's fine too.*   Now I ask you: why does a
  man want to be a General? And I answer you: because he can
  drive anywhere in Russia—with postillions and adjutants rush-
  ing on ahead to get him his next team of horses. They won't
  give them to anyone else. To a General, *everyone* has to defer:
  Councillors, Captains . . . Governors. But do you—the General—give a hoot in hell? No, for you are driving to a dinner at
  the Lord Lieutenant's and, in your presence, the Governors will
  have to remain standing! *(He roars with merriment.)*

GOVERNOR'S WIFE. Your tastes are coarse, husband. Remember:
  our life will be different now. Different friends. No one like
  this Judge who talks of nothing but dogs and enjoys nothing but
  hunting rabbits. Or the Director of Charities. Ugh. Your new
  friends will be refined. High society background. I'm uneasy
  about you, I admit: you're apt to use words that are not em-
  ployed in the best of company.

GOVERNOR. Words will never hurt you: that's a proverb.

GOVERNOR'S WIFE. Petersburg is different.

GOVERNOR. Yeah, they have fish there that just melts in your
  mouth, no chewing needed.

GOVERNOR'S WIFE. *You* must get your mind off fish. In the smart-
  est house in Petersburg, that shall be ours, there'll be a *perfume*
  to the drawing room that positively makes you close your eyes.
  (She closes her eyes and sniffs.) Hm!

  (Enter SHOPKEEPERS.)

GOVERNOR. Ah, yes. How are *you*, my friends?

SHOPKEEPERS *(bowing)*. A good health to *you*, sir.

GOVERNOR. Good health to me, in jail, ha? Wasn't that where you
  were planning to put me? Behind bars? Ha? You conniving
  frauds, you hypocritical sons of bitches, may seven devils choke
  you all!

GOVERNOR'S WIFE. Anton, watch your language.

---

*The old Sykes translation ran a note stating that the two decorations were of
equal merit, but Milton Ehre's contention that blue was superior gives more
comic point to the Wife's preference.

GOVERNOR. I have some news for you. His Excellency—the Excellency you presented your petitions to—is about to marry my daughter, put that in your pipe and smoke it. And let it now be publicly stated who the cheats are in this town. Who is it gets government contracts and then defrauds the treasury by supplying rotten cloth? You're trained to it: as little boys, before you can recite a prayer, you learn to give short measure. Which enables you to empty sixteen samovars a day and grow big bellies and still have your pockets chock full of money. Dignified now. Self-satisfied. As good as the nobility. But the real nobility—*my* peers—have an education. They may get flogged at school but they learn things. And they get culture!

SHOPKEEPERS *(bowing)*. We're sorry, sir.

GOVERNOR. Sorry now, are you? And who helped you gyp the government when you charged twenty thousand for timber and supplied one hundred rubles' worth? I could have got you sent to Siberia!

ABDUL. The Devil must've tempted us, sir. We apologize. It will never happen again.

GOVERNOR. I've got the whip hand, so you grovel at my feet. Had it been the other way round, you'd have sent *me* to Siberia.

ABDUL. Please don't ruin us, sir.

GOVERNOR. "Please don't ruin us, sir." I could—But no. Let magnanimity—*grandeur* in French, I believe—let a certain *grandeur* come into its own at this appropriate moment. MY DAUGHTER IS MARRYING A NOBLEMAN! Also appropriate would be your congratulations, and not just some sugar or a bottle of wine. *Grandeur* calls for *grandeur* as deep calls unto deep! How's that for language, wife?

GOVERNOR'S WIFE. Better.

GOVERNOR. You can go.

(The SHOPKEEPERS *go. Enter the* JUDGE *and the* DIRECTOR OF CHARITIES.*)*

JUDGE. Can this be true, Anton? This extraordinary piece of good fortune?

DIRECTOR OF CHARITIES. May I congratulate you? I'm overjoyed. *(He kisses the hand of both women.* Enter* BOBCHINSKY *and* DOBCHINSKY, *pushing their way through a supposed crowd in the doorway.)*

BOBCHINSKY. I have the honor to congratulate you.

DOBCHINSKY. I have the honor to congratulate you, Anton Antonovitch.

BOBCHINSKY. On the occasion of this propitious event.

DOBCHINSKY. *Madame!*

BOBCHINSKY. *Madame!*

(As both converge on the GOVERNOR'S WIFE, *to kiss her hand, they knock their heads together.)*

DOBCHINSKY *(kissing* MARYA's *hand).* I have the honor to congratulate *you*, Marya. You will be happy. You will wear a gold dress. You will have exquisite soup to eat. You will have a *glorious* time. You—

BOBCHINSKY *(interrupting, so he too can kiss her hand).* I have the honor to congratulate you, Marya dear. May God bring you pots of money and a baby boy no larger than this *(he indicates with his hands)* and not too small to sit on your hand.

(The SUPERINTENDENT OF SCHOOLS *had entered during the foregoing, and now comes forward.**)*

SUPERINTENDENT OF SCHOOLS. May I too have the honor . . . *(He kisses the hand of both ladies. Meanwhile the* POLICE CHIEF *and the* COP *have come in. The* COP *stands behind the* POLICE CHIEF *when he presents his compliments.)*

POLICE CHIEF. On behalf of the constabulary of our town, may I add our congratulations, *madame, mademoiselle! (He kisses both. The* COP *bows low.)*

---

*Gogol did not hesitate to call on extra actors here by introducing new characters. Since this never in this world would be permitted nowadays, the script has been shortened to fit the straightened circumstances of the late 20th Century.

**Gogol adds his wife who has one long speech.

GOVERNOR. Thank you, thank you everyone! *(Calling:)* Mishka, some more chairs!

(MISHKA, *who had been offstage, brings extra chairs.*)

Everyone take a seat!

(This is done and everyone—except MISHKA *and the* COP *who stand by the doors—now sits, expectantly. The* JUDGE *is the first to take the plunge.)*

JUDGE. Now, Governor, we're agog to know how all this came about.

GOVERNOR. He just up and proposed.

GOVERNOR'S WIFE. With delicacy and restraint. "*Madame,* says he, "life is not worth a kopeck to me. I act out of regard for your qualities of mind and heart."

MARYA. *My* qualities of mind and heart. He proposed to me.

GOVERNOR'S WIFE. Don't interrupt. And when I tried to explain that we scarcely dared hope for such an honor, he fell on his knees and said, in language I cannot possibly match: "And if you don't feel the same way, I'll kill myself."

MARYA. Only it was me he said that to.

GOVERNOR'S WIFE. It was *about* you he said that.

GOVERNOR. The expression he used was: "I'll *shoot* myself."

JUDGE. Dear me.

SUPERINTENDENT OF SCHOOLS. I see the Hand of Destiny in this.

DIRECTOR OF CHARITIES. Destiny has no hands. This is the reward of pure merit! *(To himself:)* Bullshit of course. They're just lucky.

JUDGE. Anton Antonovitch, I could *sell* you that pup now, if you want. The German shepherd. Sister of—

GOVERNOR. No, no, no dogs *now!*

JUDGE. Or another one?

DIRECTOR OF CHARITIES. And where is your distinguished guest right now? There's some talk that he left.

GOVERNOR. Yes, yes, he's away for one day on business.

GOVERNOR'S WIFE. To visit his old, *very rich* uncle and ask his blessing.

GOVERNOR. To ask his blessing. *(He sneezes. Everyone says: "Bless you.")* Thanks. He'll be back tomorrow. *(He sneezes again. More blessings and on top of them all the voice of:)*

POLICE CHIEF. Long life to your honor!

BOBCHINSKY. May you find a sack of gold in the chimney and live a hundred years.

DOBCHINSKY. May God lengthen your days for centuries!

DIRECTOR OF CHARITIES *(to himself)*. May the Devil carry you off a little earlier than that.

GOVERNOR. I thank you all and wish you all the same.

GOVERNOR'S WIFE. We'll be in Petersburg from now on. This environment is too . . . rustic for us. We don't really care for it. In Petersburg my husband's going to be a General.

GOVERNOR. Going to enjoy being a General.

SUPERINTENDENT OF SCHOOLS. For a man something may be impossible, but with God all things are possible.

JUDGE. A big ship sails deep waters.

DIRECTOR OF CHARITIES *(a little too loudly)*. A well-deserved honor!

JUDGE *(to himself)*. A General's uniform on *him* will be like a saddle on a cow. But maybe he just won't make it.

DIRECTOR OF CHARITIES *(to himself)*. What next? He certainly has the conceit for it. *(To him:)* You won't forget your old friends, will you, Governor?

JUDGE. Can we come to you in case of need?

GOVERNOR. Yes, yes, I'll be doing favors for everybody!

GOVERNOR'S WIFE. A General mustn't be burdened with too many promises, however.

(The POSTMASTER *now breaks in, an open letter in his hand.)*

POSTMASTER. An amazing thing, ladies and gentlemen: this person we took for an Inspector was *not* an Inspector.

ALL. What? Not an Inspector? Whadda ya mean? *(Etcetera.)*

POSTMASTER *(nodding vigorously)*. It's in a letter.

GOVERNOR. What letter?

POSTMASTER. One of his own. The address on it caught my attention: *"Post Office Street,* Petersburg." I smelled a rat. Someone was telling the authorities something. So I unsealed it.

GOVERNOR. That was wrong.

POSTMASTER. I know. But something got into me. I'd been on the point of despatching it, and by special delivery too. But something got into me. The desire for knowledge.

SUPERINTENDENT OF SCHOOLS. The knowledge of good and evil. Like Adam and Eve.

GOVERNOR. Opening mail is one thing. Opening the mail of an illustrious personage is another. And opening the mail of a Government Inspector is high treason.

POSTMASTER. That's just it, though. He is not an Inspector. He is not an illustrious personage.

GOVERNOR. Who in God's name is he, then—according to you?

POSTMASTER. A nobody. Nobody at all.

GOVERNOR. I won't have it. My man, you are under arrest! *(He is starting to give the signal to the* COP *when the* POSTMASTER *continues:)*

POSTMASTER. No, no, you haven't read the letter.

GOVERNOR. Don't you know this man is about to marry my daughter and I'm going to be an illustrious personage myself and send you to Siberia?

POSTMASTER. I'd better read it to you.

ALL. Do! Read it, read it for God's sake!

POSTMASTER *(reading).* "My dear Tryapitchkin, I hasten to report a marvellous adventure. On the way, I was cleaned out by an infantry captain. I was so broke, the innkeeper here was going to send me to jail. But then, on account of my Petersburg get-up, the whole town decided I was a Government Inspector, so I am now staying in the Governor's house flirting with his wife and daughter, both at the same time. Don't know which to start on first, maybe the mother: she seems more than ready to go all the way. Remember how hard up we were in Petersburg sometimes? Remember that baker who threw us out for charging our porkpies to the King of England? Well, now they lend me all the money I ask for. Would you like to put my story into one of your funny newspaper sketches? First, the Governor, stupid as the old grey mare—"

GOVERNOR. No! That's not in there!

POSTMASTER *(showing him the place)*. See for yourself.

GOVERNOR *(reading)*. "As the old grey mare." You wrote that yourself.

POSTMASTER. How could I?

DIRECTOR OF CHARITIES. Read on.

SUPERINTENDENT OF SCHOOLS. Keep going.

POSTMASTER *(continuing)*. "Stupid as the old grey mare."

GOVERNOR. You needn't keep repeating that.

POSTMASTER *(looking for his place)*. " . . . old grey mare. The Postmaster is a good sort of chap who . . ." No, here he says something improper.

GOVERNOR. Read it.

POSTMASTER. Something improper? Indecent?

GOVERNOR. Yeah. Read it. Read it *all*.

DIRECTOR OF CHARITIES *(putting his glasses on)*. I'll read it. *(Taking the letter:)* "The Postmaster is a good sort of chap who reminds me of that awful porter at the office in Petersburg; he must be an out and out drunk."

POSTMASTER *(to the audience)*. He himself is a nasty young scamp.

DIRECTOR OF CHARITIES. "The Director of Charities for his part . . ." *(He stops.)*

POLICE CHIEF.* Why've you stopped?

DIRECTOR OF CHARITIES. He's a scoundrel all right. I can't make this passage out—

POLICE CHIEF. Maybe *I* can figure it.

DIRECTOR OF CHARITIES. It gets clearer later on. I'll skip that.

POSTMASTER. No, you must read it all.

---

*The Police Chief is given the lines of a Gogol character omitted from this version.

ALL. Give it up! Give it to him. *(Etcetera.)*

POLICE CHIEF *(having got the letter).* "The Director of Charities for his part is just a *pig* in a skull cap . . ."

DIRECTOR OF CHARITIES. Pigs don't wear skull caps.

POLICE CHIEF. "The Superintendent of Schools reeks of onions."

SUPERINTENDENT OF SCHOOLS *(to the audience).* That's an outright lie. I never touch onions.

JUDGE. Thank God he has nothing on me.

POLICE CHIEF. "As for the Judge . . ."

JUDGE. Stop! This letter is tedious. Let's drop it.

SUPERINTENDENT OF SCHOOLS. Not now, not now!

POSTMASTER. Read on.

DIRECTOR OF CHARITIES. Read on.

POLICE CHIEF. "As for the Judge, he is simply *mo-vaze tone.*" Is that French?

JUDGE. God knows. I just hope it isn't dirty.

POLICE CHIEF. "Still, their hospitality was wonderful. They're nice guys, really. But I must find a better way of spending my time. Shall I follow you into the Literary Life, dear Tryapitchkin? Write me in Saratov." *(He turns the letter over to read the address:)* It's addressed to "Tryapitchkin, 3rd floor, 97 Post Office Street, Petersburg."

GOVERNOR. I'm seeing red. I'm seeing pigs' snouts instead of faces. He is killing me. Bring him back this minute!

POSTMASTER. He was given the fastest horses we had. With orders ahead to the other posting-stations.

JUDGE. And the fellow borrowed three hundred rubles from me.

SUPERINTENDENT OF SCHOOLS. Three hundred from me too.

POSTMASTER. And from me.

BOBCHINSKY. From me and Pyotr Ivanovitch, sixty-five.

JUDGE. How on earth can all this have occurred?

GOVERNOR *(slapping his brow).* I've been in government service thirty years. Not a merchant, not a contractor, ever got the better of me. Rogues? I know rogues: I've beaten them all at their own game. Cheats and scoundrels who'd been swindling the whole world were caught—by me. I've even hoodwinked three Lieutenant-Generals.

GOVERNOR'S WIFE. Anyway, it's impossible, he's engaged to Marya.

GOVERNOR. You're an idiot. But I'm a worse idiot. To take a rag of a man like that, a mere milksop, for an illustrious personage! Bells jingling, flags flying, he is now busy spreading this tale across the entire country. I shall be *written about* in Petersburg: it's not enough to be a laughingstock in your hometown, they have to put you in a farce in the nation's capital! A ghastly thing like this happens and *the whole world* laughs! *(To the audience:)* What are *you* laughing at? You are laughing at yourselves. *(He stamps on the floor.)* Very well. I'll get back at these damn liberals, I'll tie them all in a knot, I'll pound them all to a jelly! *(Again, he stamps on the floor.)* Whom God would punish, he first makes mad. What was there that resembled an Inspector in that little twirp? Yet I and everyone—Explain it to me.

DIRECTOR OF CHARITIES. The Devil was in it.

JUDGE. We have to ask who started it. Well, *they* did. *(He points at* DOBCHINSKY *and* BOBCHINSKY.)*

BOBCHINSKY. I never dreamed of such a thing.

DOBCHINSKY. I had nothing to do with it.

DIRECTOR OF CHARITIES. It *was* your doing.

SUPERINTENDENT OF SCHOOLS. Certainly it was. They came running from the inn. It was they who found him.

GOVERNOR. That's right. It *was* you.

DIRECTOR OF CHARITIES. Devil take you.

GOVERNOR. You confuse people's brains. You spread gossip. You—

JUDGE. You have smutty minds!

SUPERINTENDENT OF SCHOOLS. You're morons!

DIRECTOR OF CHARITIES. Fat little nothings.

(All surround DOBCHINSKY *and* BOBCHINSKY.)*

BOBCHINSKY. It wasn't me. It was Pyotr Ivanovitch!

DOBCHINSKY. Aw, no, no, no. *You* started it—

BOBCHINSKY. No, *you* did—

(*Enter a Gendarme.*)*

GENDARME. The Inspector authorized by the Imperial government has arrived in town. Requesting your immediate presence, he awaits you at the inn.

These words fall like a thunderbolt. An exclamation of astonishment rises to the lips of the ladies, and the whole group, changing their present stances, now are petrified.

TABLEAU VIVANT

In the middle, the GOVERNOR, *like a post, arms outstretched, head flung back. On his right, his wife and daughter leaning toward him with a vehement expression. Behind them, the* POSTMASTER *has become a question mark addressed to the audience. The* SUPER-INTENDENT OF SCHOOLS *is beside him in a state of innocent bewilderment. On the* GOVERNOR'*s left stands the* DIRECTOR OF CHARITIES, *his head turned to one side as though he's listening to something. Next to him, the* JUDGE, *his hands flung outward and almost squatting on the floor, his lips in a whistling position and seeming about to say, "Here's a pretty how d'ye do!" At the edge of the stage,* BOBCHINSKY *and* DOBCHINSKY, *staring at each other with their mouths open and their hands stretched out toward each other. All others just like posts. The petrified group remains in position almost a minute and a half.***

---

*According to Milton Ehre, he is a member of a secret police force established by Tsar Nicholas I. If, however, as in all Russian productions, he is in uniform it would not seem that his functions are very secret.

**Gogol's own description of the famous Tableau Vivant has not been tempered with except in the omission of characters not present in this version.

GAMBLERS

A Comedy in One Act

Paul Sylbert's design for the Bentley production of *Gamblers*. Reproduced by permission of Paul Sylbert.

Enter IHAREV, *accompanied by* ALEXEY.

ALEXEY. Please come in, sir. *(*IHAREV *hesitates.)* Nice little room, sir.

IHAREV. Huh?

ALEXEY. Quiet. No noise at all, sir.

IHAREV. No noise? *(Points to bed.)* How about the imperial cavalry?

ALEXEY. Fleas, sir? If you're bitten by fleas, we take the full responsibility, sir.

IHAREV *(to* GAVROOSHKA *who is offstage).* Bring the things from the carriage, Gavrooshka. What's your name, my good man? *(Hangs up coat upper left.)*

ALEXEY. Alexey, sir.

IHAREV. I'm Mr. Iharev. Who's staying here right now?

ALEXEY. Oh, a lot of people, sir.

IHAREV. Such as?

ALEXEY. Such as Mr. Ootesh, sir. Such as Colonel Krugel, sir. Such as Mr. Shonev, sir.

IHAREV. Do they, um, play cards?

ALEXEY. They've been playing for six solid nights, sir.

IHAREV. Here's a couple of rubles.

ALEXEY *(bowing).* Much obliged, I'm sure, sir.

IHAREV. There's more where that came from.

ALEXEY. Glad to hear it, sir.

IHAREV. Do they, um, play—among themselves?

ALEXEY. No, sir. Oh no, sir. First they played with Lieutenant Artunovsky—but he lost all his money, sir.

IHAREV. Ah!

ALEXEY. Then they won thirty-six thousand from Prince Shenkin.

IHAREV. Here's another ten rubles. Did *you* buy the cards?

ALEXEY. No, they did, sir.

IHAREV. Where?

ALEXEY. From the local store, sir.

IHAREV. What?

ALEXEY. From the local store, sir.

IHAREV. That's a lie, my good man.

ALEXEY. No, really, sir! Oh no! *(A knock.)*

IHAREV. Let's see who this is. *(Enter* GAVROOSHKA.*)* Ah, Gavrooshka, at last! Alexey, I want you to meet Gavrooshka, my valet. You might like to fraternize with him. In the meantime, get moving, both of you and bring me some shaving water and a towel. Be back in the twinkling of an eye. *(Exeunt both servants.* IHAREV *opens suitcase filled with decks of cards.)* Aren't they lovely? Every deck worth its weight in gold! Every deck earned by the sweat of my brow! My eyes are still weak from studying the markings on the back. But what a sound investment! What a dowry for my daughters! What a start in life for my sons! Look at this deck. I should call it the pearl of great price. No, it's more . . . human than that . . . I shall call it Adelaide. Adelaide, darling, be faithful to me, won't you? Like your little sister here that won me a cool eighty thousand? Only be faithful, Adelaide, and when we get home, I'll have a monument built in your honor—real Moscow marble . . . *(He quickly closes the box. Enter* ALEXEY *and* GAVROOSHKA *with shaving water and towel.)* Where are those gentlemen? Are they in?

ALEXEY. Yes, they are in the lounge, sir.

IHAREV. I'll go look them over. *(Exit* IHAREV.*)*

ALEXEY *(seats* GAVROOSHKA*)*. Hey! You come far?

GAVROOSHKA. From Ryazan.

ALEXEY. That your home?

GAVROOSHKA. No, we're from Smolensk province.

ALEXEY. Smolensk. Nice place to live?

GAVROOSHKA. I wouldn't know.

ALEXEY. Huh?

GAVROOSHKA. He just owns it, he don't live there.

ALEXEY. An estate, huh?

GAVROOSHKA. Two estates. One in Smolensk province, one in Kaluga province.

ALEXEY. Hm. Quite a set-up.

GAVROOSHKA. Sure. Owns a hundred and eighty serfs. In the Smolensk house there's Ignaty the butler, Pavlooshka who used to travel with the master, Gerasim the footman, Ivan another footman, *(Enter* KRUGEL *and* SHONEV.*)* Ivan the kennel-boy, Ivan again who plays in the band, the cook Grigory, the cook Semyon, Baruch the gardener, Dementy the coachman. . . .

SHONEV. You don't think he'll notice, this Mr. Iharev?

KRUGEL. Of course not. Ootesh will keep him busy. *(To* ALEXEY.*)* Run along, boy, they're calling you. *(Exit* ALEXEY.*)* As for you, my good man, where does your master come from?

GAVROOSHKA. Right now . . . from Ryazan, sir. *(Tries to rise —is pushed down.)*

KRUGEL. He's a landowner, is he?

GAVROOSHKA. Yes, sir.

KRUGEL. Does he, um, play cards?

GAVROOSHKA. Yes, sir.

KRUGEL *(to* SHONEV*).* Give him a little something. *(*SHONEV *gives him money.)*

SHONEV. Now tell all!

GAVROOSHKA. You won't tell him I told you?

SHONEV. Really!

KRUGEL. A soldier's word is his bond.

SHONEV. How is he doing?

KRUGEL. Has he been winning?

GAVROOSHKA. Why? You know Colonel Chebotarev?

SHONEV. Colonel who?

KRUGEL. Why?

GAVROOSHKA. We cleaned him out three weeks ago, sir. Eighty thousand rubles, a Warsaw carriage, a box, a rug, gold epaulettes . . . the gold alone was worth six hundred rubles.

KRUGEL *(to* SHONEV*).* Eighty thousand rubles? *(*SHONEV *shakes his head.)* Sounds fishy, huh? We'll soon find out. *(To* GAVROOSHKA.*)* Tell me, my good man, when your master stays home, what does he do?

GAVROOSHKA. What does he do? Why he's a gentleman, he does nothing.

KRUGEL. You're lying.

SHONEV. I bet he plays cards the whole damn time.

GAVROOSHKA. Well, I've only been traveling with him two weeks. He always took Pavlooshka. There's Gerasim the footman, Ivan another footman, Ivan the kennel boy, another Ivan who plays in the band. . .

SHONEV *(to* KRUGEL*).* Think he's a professional?

KRUGEL. Most likely.

SHONEV. What shall we do?

KRUGEL. What do we always do? Give it a try, man, give it a try! *(They leave.)*

GAVROOSHKA. Pretty tricky, aren't they? See this money? Gonna come in handy. Enough to buy a bonnet for Masha, some candy for the kids. Hey, I like this travel stuff. For one thing, every time he sends you on an errand, you can keep some of the change. A gentleman's life for me! Go where you like when you like! You're tired of Smolensk, so what the hell, you go to Ryazan. You're tired of Ryazan, so you go to Kazan, you're tired of Kazan so . . . got it? Now, which is more deestangay . . . Kazan or Ryazan? Huh? Whadja say? Sure, I guess Kazan'd be more deestangay 'cause . . . *(Enter* IHAREV.*)*

IHAREV. There's nothing special about them I think. And yet, how I should love to clean them out! Holy St. Nicolas, how I should love it! My hand keeps shaking. I can't shave properly.

ALEXEY *(entering).* Shall I bring your worship something to eat?

IHAREV. Yes, lunch for four. Caviar, smoked salmon, and four bottles of wine. And feed *him.*

ALEXEY *(to* GAVROOSHKA*).* Go into the kitchen, it's all ready. *(Exit* GAVROOSHKA.*)*

IHAREV. How much did they slip you?

ALEXEY. Who, sir?

IHAREV. Oh, come on.

ALEXEY. They did slip me something, sir.

IHAREV. Fifty rubles?

ALEXEY. Yes, sir, fifty rubles.

IHAREV. On that table is a hundred ruble bill. Take it. Go on. What are you afraid of? It won't bite you. I ask nothing in return except honesty. I want you to be honest with me, understand? Whether the cards come from the local store is none of my business. Here's a packet of one dozen. Do we understand each other?

ALEXEY. Oh yes, sir. Yes sir.

IHAREV. Then put them out of sight for a while, huh? *(Exit ALEXEY.)* Eighty thousand rubles. I'll show them! *(Enter SHONEV and KRUGEL.)*

IHAREV. Come in, gentlemen. You must excuse me, gentlemen. Nothing but four chairs. The room is simple. *(Enter OOTESH.)* Mr. Ootesh!

OOTESH. A warm welcome from the host is better than the finest luxury, Mr. Iharev. *(He sits.)*

IHAREV. Colonel Krugel.

KRUGEL. In the army, we never judge a man by his circumstances, Mr. Iharev. *(Sits.)*

IHAREV. Mr. Shonev!

SHONEV. It's never the room that matters but the company, Mr. Iharev. *(Sits.) Vive la compagnie!*

OOTESH. I agree! Without company, I can't exist. Remember how I came here, Krugel, all alone? Didn't know a soul. The landlady an old woman! On the stairs, a chambermaid with a face like a turnip! I see an infantry officer trailing her, thankful for small mercies . . . Deadly! But then, fate brought Colonel Krugel along! And Mr. Shonev!

KRUGEL. Was I pleased!

SHONEV. Was I pleased!

OOTESH. I can't exist without company—not for a day, not for an hour. I have to open my heart to everyone I meet.

KRUGEL. That's bad.

OOTESH. Bad?

SHONEV. All excess is bad.

KRUGEL. Besides, don't you often get played for a sucker?

OOTESH. Always! Invariably! But I just can't help myself.

KRUGEL. Well, that's beyond me—being open with *everyone*. Friends, of course, are a different matter.

OOTESH. But man belongs to society.

KRUGEL. Not the whole of him.

OOTESH. The whole of him.

KRUGEL. Not the whole of him, Ootesh.

OOTESH. Yes, the whole of him, Krugel.

KRUGEL. No, no, not the whole of him, Ootesh.

OOTESH. Yes, yes, the whole of him, Krugel.

SHONEV. Don't argue when you're wrong, Ootesh.

OOTESH. I'll prove it, Shonev. Why, it's a duty. It's moral . . . it's a moral obligation! It's . . .

SHONEV. He's off again! Amazing how worked up he gets. You can make sense of the first three words, but after that . . . *oh, là, là!*

OOTESH. I can't help myself. When it's a question of principle, I don't know what I'm saying. I have to warn people. "If anything of the sort is discussed," I have to say, "You must excuse me, but my feelings will run away with me. My blood will boil."

IHAREV *(to the audience)*. His blood will boil, all right, but not for that reason. *(Aloud.)* Well, gentlemen, while we're discussing our moral obligations, how about a little game of Bank?*

OOTESH. By all means!

SHONEV. Provided, of course, that it's not for high stakes.

KRUGEL. I'm never against a little innocent merriment.

IHAREV. What about the cards? *(Pause.)* I assume we can get some on the premises?

---

*The Gogol scholar Leon Stilman reports that the game called in Russian banchik or banchók denoted different games at different times but is here, as in Pushkin's *Queen of Spades*, a variant of Faro. As the word Faro says very little to a modern English-speaking audience, the present adapter has preferred to let the game be called Bank, not just because that is its name in Russian, but because of the role of banks in this play.

SHONEV. You've only to ask for them, Mr. Iharev.

IHAREV *(claps his hands)*. Alexey! Cards! *(*ALEXEY *brings cards and food.)* And meanwhile, gentlemen, may I offer you . . . ? The smoked salmon's nothing special but the caviar's not bad.

KRUGEL *(eating)*. Why, the smoked salmon's good!

SHONEV *(eating)*. The caviar's *magnifique!*

KRUGEL. Remember the splendid cheese we had at Pyotr Alexandrovitch Alexandrov's?

SHONEV. I shall never forget the splendid cheese we had at Pyotr Alexandrovitch Alexandrov's.

IHAREV. Very well, gentlemen, the cards are on the table!

OOTESH. Cards! Just like old times!

KRUGEL. Haven't played since I left the regiment!

OOTESH. Dear old cards!

SHONEV. Where are the snows of yesteryear?

IHAREV *(aside)*. What a load of bull!

OOTESH. Would you like to hold the bank, Mr. Iharev?

IHAREV. By all means. Uh, uh. Five hundred rubles. A nice little bank! Cut! *(He deals and the game is played.)*

KRUGEL. Just a minute! There should be two threes left in this deck.

OOTESH. There's something wrong. Those aren't our cards. *(The game goes on)*.

IHAREV *(to* SHONEV*)*. How about you, Mr. Shonev? Aren't you betting?

SHONEV. Let me sit out this round. *(To* OOTESH.*)* He's cheating like crazy. He's a professional from way back.

OOTESH. We can't pass up the eighty thousand, can we?

KRUGEL. We may have to.

OOTESH. Well, that's the question. Meanwhile . . .

KRUGEL. What?

SHONEV. What?

OOTESH. We must tell him.

KRUGEL. Tell him?

SHONEV. What for?

OOTESH. I'll explain later. Help me. Mr. Iharev, we have a little secret to tell you.

IHAREV. What can I do for you, Mr. Ootesh?

OOTESH. It's no use.

KRUGEL. No use, old man!

SHONEV. No use at all.

IHAREV. How so?

OOTESH. What's the good of talking? A fellow knows his own sort.

IHAREV. I'm not sure I know what you mean, Mr. Ootesh.

KRUGEL. We recognize your skill, Mr. Iharev.

SHONEV. We can do justice to your accomplishments.

OOTESH. And so, in the name of my comrades and myself, I wish to propose—friendly alliance.

KRUGEL. Pool our capital.

SHONEV. Combine our brains.

IHAREV. Why should I believe you, Mr. Ootesh?

OOTESH. Forgive us, Mr. Iharev. We took you for just an average man.

KRUGEL. We were wrong.

SHONEV. You're one of us.

OOTESH. Accept our friendship.

IHAREV. Very well. Very well, it's a deal.

OOTESH. Shake!

KRUGEL. Shake!

SHONEV. Shake!

OOTESH. Pretence and ceremony adieu! Let us adjourn to the conference table. *(They sit.)* How long have you studied the . . . higher mysteries, Mr. Iharev?

IHAREV. I had the call pretty early in life, Mr. Ootesh. I used to hold the bank under my desk in high school.

OOTESH. There's nothing like education, is there, Krugel? Remember that extraordinary child, Shonev?

IHAREV. What child was that, Mr. Shonev?

OOTESH. Tell him.

KRUGEL. Tell him, Shonev.

SHONEV. I shall never forget it. Mr. Ootesh's brother-in-law said to me: "Would you like to see a prodigy? A boy of eleven, the son of Ivan Kubyshev, can fool with cards better than any professional. Go see for yourself." I went to the house. A middle-aged man came to the door. I said, "Excuse me, I hear that God has blessed you with a son of unusual talent." "I can't deny it" he replied with pleasing modesty. "Though it is not for me to sing the praises of my own son, he is a prodigy. Misha!" he said, "show our visitor what you can do." The boy was a mere infant, no higher than my elbow. But when he dealt the cards, I was flabbergasted.

IHAREV. Could you tell how he did it? (SHONEV *shakes his head twice*.) Extraordinary!

OOTESH. A phenomenon.

KRUGEL. An infant phenomenon.

IHAREV. When you think what skill it takes. To study the markings on the cards . . .

OOTESH. Marking cards is old-fashioned. We just study the key.

IHAREV. The key of the pattern?

OOTESH. The pattern on the back. In a town I mustn't mention by name there's a worthy man who does nothing else. Every year he gets several hundred decks from Moscow—from whom, is a matter wrapped in obscurity—his job is to analyze the pattern on each card and send out the key. He gets five thousand a year for it.

IHAREV. Must be a difficult job.

OOTESH. Someone has to do it. Division of labour, hm? Take a carriage-builder—he doesn't build the whole carriage himself; he hands over part of the job to the blacksmith, part to the upholsterer . . .

IHAREV. One question. How do you make sure your own decks are used? You can't always bribe a servant.

KRUGEL. God forbid!

SHONEV. Besides, it's risky.

OOTESH. No, no. Remember how we went to work that time, Krugel?

SHONEV. Oh, that was *délicieux*.

IHAREV. How *was* it, Colonel?

OOTESH. Tell him.

KRUGEL. It was like this. Our agent arrives at a market, passes himself off as a tradesman, stays at the inn, hasn't time to set up a stall, just stays at the inn, eating, drinking, running up a bill, then he suddenly disappears without paying. The innkeeper ransacks his room, finds a package, undoes it, a hundred little boxes fall out, in each box twelve decks of cards. He auctions them off, the local shopkeepers buy them, stock up with 'em . . . Three days later, the whole town is lamenting its losses at cards.

IHAREV. Very neat.

KRUGEL. Then there was that other fellow.

SHONEV. The country gentleman.

IHAREV. How was it with him, Mr. Ootesh?

OOTESH. That wasn't bad either. I don't know whether you know him. Arkády Dergunov? A man of means. First rate card player, but honest. There's no way of getting at him; he takes care of everything, even his servants are honest, his household is a regular beehive, his estate, his parks are all in the English style. A gentleman, you might say, in the best sense of the word . . . Well, we thought of a plan. One morning, a cart dashes by with a lot of young fellows on it, drunk, bawling songs, drinking like mad. The servants come out to look, the way they do, gaping and laughing. Then they notice something has dropped off the cart, they run up, and find a bag. They wave and shout "Stop," but no one takes any notice. The cart rushes ahead in a cloud of dust. They undo the bag, find clothes of some sort, two hundred rubles, and forty dozen decks of cards. Well, naturally, they don't throw the money down the drain and as for the cards, they find their way into the master's own tables. Next evening—when the game is done—Arkady Dergunov is left without a kopeck.

IHAREV. Pretty smart! Some people would have a name for that, but we know, well, there's something fine about it; as you say, it's a higher mystery.

OOTESH. It's a discipline.

SHONEV. And no respecter of persons!

OOTESH. It's a duty.

KRUGEL. It imposes harsh responsibilities!

OOTESH. Why, if I sat down to play with my own father, you know what I'd have to do?

SHONEV. Cheat him!

OOTESH. Cheat my own father.

KRUGEL. Gambling is the great leveller.

OOTESH. All men are equal—at cards.

IHAREV. Very true. People won't understand that a gambler may be the noblest of men. I know one—oh, a very clever fellow at cards—but would that stop him giving his last ruble to a beggar?

OOTESH. Of course not.

IHAREV. Let me put a case. If you had two buddies, and the three of you played together, but the fourth player wasn't a buddy, wouldn't you have to be loyal to your two buddies, even if the fourth player was your grandmother?

OOTESH. Certainly.

IHAREV. Like in a civil war, huh? Father against son, son against granny, but all in a great cause, correct?

OOTESH. Correct.

KRUGEL. Correct.

SHONEV. Correct.

IHAREV. So that's settled. Now I want you to see a little action. But first, tell me, do you know what a made-up deck is?

OOTESH. Oh, I think so. Isn't it when you can guess any card at a distance?

IHAREV. I have my own system. Nearly six months' work. Couldn't bear the sunlight for a week afterwards. The doctor said I had inflammation of the eyes. *(Takes out a deck from the box.)* Here she is! You may think it foolish, but this deck has a name. She's human.

OOTESH. Really?

KRUGEL. Human?

SHONEV. *La comédie humaine.*

IHAREV. She's called Adelaide.

OOTESH. Hear that, everybody? This deck's called Adelaide!

KRUGEL. Well!

SHONEV. Glad to meet you, Adelaide!

OOTESH. This is something! Can you really identify any card at a distance?

IHAREV. Try me. I'll stand five paces away and name every card. Two thousand rubles if I fail.

OOTESH. Very well. What card is this?

IHAREV. A seven.

OOTESH. Right. And this one?

IHAREV. A jack.

OOTESH. Good God! And this one?

IHAREV. A three.

OOTESH. Incredible.

KRUGEL. Incredible.

SHONEV. Absolutely *incroyable*.

OOTESH. Let me take another look. *(Examines the cards.)* Adelaide! Well, she deserves a name. Though, of course, she's rather hard to make use of. You'd have to slip her on to the table yourself.

IHAREV. I do it in the heat of the game when the stakes are so high that even the most hardened veteran is all worked up. When a man's been playing for six solid nights, you know how it is . . . he plays himself silly, and in the heat of the game I change the cards.

OOTESH. How do you do that, Mr. Iharev?

IHAREV. It's a matter of keeping cool when the other fellows are steamed up. As you know there are thousands of ways of distracting attention: take issue with one of the players, say his score's been put down wrong, all eyes turn to him, and . . . *(gesture.)*

OOTESH. Wonderful! To your other accomplishments, you add the priceless gift of keeping cool. Association with you will be of value to us, Mr. Iharev. And so . . .

KRUGEL. With no more ado . . .

SHONEV. Let us declare ourselves . . . comrades.

IHAREV. Agreed.

OOTESH. We must drink on it. *(He pours wine.)* To a friendly collaboration.

IHAREV. To a friendly collaboration.

KRUGEL. Hip hip—

SHONEV. Hooray.

KRUGEL. Hip hip . . .

SHONEV. Hooray!

KRUGEL. Hip hip . . .

SHONEV. Hooray! *(They drink.)*

OOTESH. Well, here we are.

KRUGEL. Mobilized for battle.

SHONEV. Weapons in hand . . .

KRUGEL. Our morale sky-high . . .

IHAREV. But no enemy!

OOTESH. That's right. No enemy. *(To* KRUGEL.*)* What do you say? You know of one?

KRUGEL. Maybe.

OOTESH. How about you?

SHONEV. *Peut-être.*

OOTESH. I know who you mean.

IHAREV. Who? Who? Who is it?

OOTESH. Nothing doing. There's a country gentleman staying here, a Mr. Glov. But what's the good of talking about him? He doesn't play cards. We've tried . . . I've been at him for a month.

KRUGEL. We have his confidence.

SHONEV. We have his affection.

OOTESH. But we don't have *him.*

IHAREV. Supposing *I* try? You never can tell.

OOTESH. I can. I can tell you right now. You can save your breath to cool your porridge.

IHAREV. Oh, come on, let's try.

KRUGEL. There's no harm in bringing him in.

SHONEV. No harm at all in bringing him in.

OOTESH. All right, I don't really mind, I'll bring him in.

IHAREV. Oh, good!

OOTESH. I'll be right back. *(Exit OOTESH.)*

IHAREV. You never can tell. That's what I always say. Sometimes a thing seems out of the question . . .

SHONEV. I agree. Man is not God. Man is, um . . . man, do you agree? He may say "no" today, he may say "no" tomorrow, he may say "no" the day after tomorrow, but on the fourth day, if you tackle him properly, he'll say "yes."

KRUGEL. Only this man isn't like that.

IHAREV. Oh, Colonel Krugel, we must hope you're wrong. Oh, how I long to get back to work! Good hard work! There's nothing like it. I won eighty thousand . . .

KRUGEL. Eighty thousand?

SHONEV. Eighty thousand?

IHAREV. . . . from Colonel Chebotarov last month. Since then, I've been unemployed. I can't tell you how bored I've been.

SHONEV. I understand. It's the way a general must feel when there's no war on: waiting . . . hoping . . .

IHAREV. You get so distraught, you'd sit down and play with kids for five rubles.

SHONEV. It's natural. You get in such a state you play with the wrong people. You even forget to win.

IHAREV. Is he very rich, this Glov?

KRUGEL. Oh, he has money.

SHONEV. He owns about a thousand serfs.

IHAREV. I'll be damned. Shall we get him drunk? Send for Champagne? Alexey!

KRUGEL. He never touches a drop.

IHAREV. What can we do? Oh, wait a minute . . . cards are tempting things. Suppose he just saw us playing . . .

KRUGEL. What do you think? Shall we try it?

SHONEV. Ye-e-s. We may as well try it.

KRUGEL. Shonev and I'll be having a small game for low stakes over here . . . You talk to him over there.

SHONEV. But don't lay it on too thick. Old men are suspicious. *(Enter* OOTESH *and* GLOV, *an elderly man.)*

OOTESH. Mr. Iharev, let me introduce . . . Mr. Glov.

IHAREV. I have long been desirous of the honour . . .

GLOV. I am pleased to make your acquaintance, sir. I only regret that it is just as I am leaving.

IHAREV. Please sit down, Mr. Glov. Have you been here long?

GLOV. Ah, Mr. Iharev, how sick I am of this town. I shall be thankful body and soul to get out of it as quickly as possible.

IHAREV. You are detained by business, Mr. Glov?

GLOV. Yes, Mr. Iharev. And troublesome business too.

IHAREV. A lawsuit I presume, Mr. Glov?

GLOV. No, no, it's not quite that bad. I am marrying off my daughter, sir, she's eighteen. I've come here to raise a mortgage on my estate. It would all have been arranged long ago but the bank hasn't paid up yet. I am waiting, Mr. Iharev.

IHAREV. May I ask for what sum you are mortgaging your estate, Mr. Glov?

GLOV. Two hundred thousand rubles.

IHAREV. Two hundred thousand rubles?

GLOV. They should pay up any day, but it keeps dragging on, and with the wedding and all . . . Everything is held up . . . so I've decided not to wait any longer.

IHAREV. You won't wait for your money, Mr. Glov?

GLOV. What am I to do? It's a month now since I've seen my wife and children. I don't even get letters, God knows what is going on. I'm leaving the mortgage business to my son who will stay here. *(To* SHONEV *and* KRUGEL.) But I believe I am interrupting you gentlemen.

KRUGEL. Not at all. Just a little game to pass the time.

GLOV. The game of Bank, Colonel Krugel?

KRUGEL. Bank!

SHONEV. Can you call it Bank when you play for one ruble stakes?

GLOV. Ah, my friends, listen to an old man. Of course there is no harm in it, and you can't lose much, but yet ... ah, gentlemen, I've played myself, and I know from experience: everything in this world begins in a small way, but many, many things end in a big way.

OOTESH. Watch this, Mr. Iharev.

KRUGEL. Mr. Glov, you old folks make a mountain out of a molehill.

SHONEV. Sit down, Mr. Glov.

GLOV. I'm not so old, Colonel. I go by experience.

KRUGEL. I speak of old people in general, Mr. Glov. If they burn their fingers, they are sure everyone else will too.

SHONEV. If a man is bitten by a dog on the main street, all dogs bite, and we must all keep away from the main street.

GLOV. True, on the one hand, there is that failing; but, on the other, look at the young folks! They are too reckless. They may break their necks at any minute.

KRUGEL. Also true! One never finds a happy medium.

SHONEV. When a man is young he is so wild he is insufferable. When he is old he plays the saint and becomes insufferable once again.

GLOV. True! How true!

OOTESH. Speaking of cards, I agree with Mr. Glov. I used to play myself. But I'm thankful to say I have given it up. Not because I lost money or thought fate was against me. I assure you that's of no consequence. What is the loss of money to the loss of one's peace of mind? The worry of gambling, the strain, the wear and tear, they take years off a man's life.

GLOV. That is so, Mr. Ootesh. A very wise observation. May I ask an indiscreet question?

OOTESH. Pray do.

GLOV. May I ask, though it is a delicate subject, and I haven't known you very long—how old are you, Mr. Ootesh?

OOTESH. Thirty-nine, Mr. Glov.

GLOV. Thirty-nine. A young, young man. Oh, if only we had more men in Russia like him. So wise! So mature! The golden age would return! How privileged I am to have made your acquaintance.

IHAREV. And I agree with him. My children will never touch a deck of cards! Of course, with grown-ups, it's a little different. And with older grown-ups, poor things, they can't dance, they can't sing, they can't . . .

GLOV. True! How true! An old man's round of pleasure is small, but dear sirs, there are other things in life. There are sacred duties to perform. Mr. Iharev is young. He hasn't yet known the one true happiness—a father's happiness in a Christian home. How I long for the moment of my homecoming! "Papa, dear Papa is home," my daughter will cry. "Papa, dear Papa," my little boy will echo. *(SHONEV registers interest.)* Yes, he'll be back from private school. I haven't seen him in six months . . . What bliss, Mr. Ootesh, and what balm to the aching heart. After that, can I sink to this?

IHAREV. Well, paternal feelings are one thing, playing cards is another. Why should they get in each other's way? What *I* ask myself is this—

(Enter ALEXEY.)

ALEXEY. The horses are ready, Mr. Glov. Your man's asking about the trunks. Should he take them out?

GLOV. I'll be right there. Excuse me a moment, gentlemen. *(Exit with ALEXEY.)*

IHAREV. It's no use.

OOTESH. Didn't I tell you? You only have to take one look at him . . .

IHAREV. Still, we could have tried. Why did you have to back him up?

OOTESH. With men like that, you've got to be subtle, my dear Iharev.

IHAREV. So you were subtle, and he's leaving.

OOTESH. The end, my friend, is not yet. He laughs best who laughs last. All's well that ends well. *(Enter GLOV.)* See what I mean?

GLOV. I came back—to thank you all for the pleasure of your company. I am sorry not to have made your acquaintance earlier in life. Maybe God will bring us together again.

OOTESH. It's a small world.

KRUGEL. Tiny.

SHONEV. Infinitesimal.

GLOV. How true! We may meet next year, next month, tomorrow afternoon. Good-bye, gentlemen. And I thank you. Above all I thank you, Mr. Ootesh, you broke through the wall of an old man's solitude.

OOTESH. One does what one can.

KRUGEL. Little though it may be.

SHONEV. No man can do more.

GLOV. May I ask one little favor, Mr. Ootesh?

OOTESH. We are all at your service, Mr. Glov.

KRUGEL. At all times, Mr. Glov.

SHONEV. *Toujours la politesse,* Mr. Glov.

GLOV. No, I shouldn't have suggested it.

OOTESH. Yes, please, I insist. Yes.

GLOV. It's Sasha. My little boy. (SHONEV *registers interest.*) Not the one in school, the one here with me. He's twenty-two, poor little thing. He's finished college and now he wants to join the Hussars. (KRUGEL *registers interest.*) Yes, the Hussars. I say to him: "Sasha," I say, "Sasha, it's early days. How do you know you'd *like* the Hussars? How about the Civil Service?" But you know how children are. It's the gold braid, the white uniform, the giant epaulets . . . so will you help a father in distress? *(Rises.)* Look after the boy for me? Shield him from the world and its ways? He has a little business to attend to here . . .

OOTESH. I'll be a second father to him, my dear Mr. Glov. *(They embrace.)*

GLOV. A friend in need. God will reward you, Mr. Ootesh. Goodbye, gentlemen, and God speed! *(Moves to the door.)*

KRUGEL. A pleasant journey to you, Mr. Glov.

SHONEV. May you find all well at home, Mr. Glov.

OOTESH. I'll help you into your carriage, Mr. Glov.

GLOV. Oh, sir, you are too kind. *(Exeunt* GLOV *and* OOTESH.*)*

IHAREV. For Christ's sake! The bird has flown!

SHONEV. A bird well worth the plucking.

IHAREV. "Two hundred thousand rubles"—how thrilling those words are!

KRUGEL. The mind likes to dwell on words like that.

IHAREV. Doesn't it, though? Just think, for instance, how much waste there is in the world, money thrown down the drain. Why should that man have two hundred thousand? What for? He squanders it on fripperies.

SHONEV. On mummery-flummery.

KRUGEL. It's economically unsound.

IHAREV. Money shouldn't lie rotting in banks, it's the life-blood of the social organism, it must circulate. Right?

KRUGEL. Right.

SHONEV. Right.

IHAREV. And why should a single man want all the money in the world? For my part, I'd be happy with that one small amount —that inconsiderable sum—now lying idle in this confounded bank.

KRUGEL. Myself, I'd be happy with half of it.

SHONEV. I might even settle for a quarter. *(OOTESH enters.)*

OOTESH. It's all right, gentlemen, everything's all right. The old fool's gone, the son remains behind.

IHAREV. But . . .

OOTESH. And you know what? The poor little thing has power of attorney to collect the money from the bank!

IHAREV. What good does that do us?

OOTESH. Why, man, I'm practically his official guardian. "Mr. Ootesh, will take care of everything," the old fool told him. Then again, Mr. Poor Little Thing is dying to be a Hussar . . . I'll show him to you. *(He rushes out.)*

IHAREV. So that was . . .

SHONEV. Three cheers for Ootesh, colleague and friend. Hip, hip . . .

KRUGEL. Hooray.

SHONEV. Hip, hip . . .

KRUGEL. Hooray.

SHONEV. Hip, hip . . .

KRUGEL. Hooray. *(They drink.)*

IHAREV. So that was why . . .

KRUGEL. Of course it was.

SHONEV. He's smart.

KRUGEL. A remarkable talent.

SHONEV. Most likely to succeed.

IHAREV. Still, when the old boy said he was leaving his son behind . . .

KRUGEL. You thought of the same thing?

IHAREV. Well, nearly.

SHONEV. That's the difference. Ootesh thought of it a hundred per cent.

IHAREV. He *is* smart.

KRUGEL. And you don't know the half of it, Mr. Iharev.

SHONEV. You don't even know the quarter of it, Mr. Iharev. *(Enter* OOTESH, *bringing* GLOV JUNIOR.)

OOTESH. Gentlemen, I want to introduce Mr. Glov Junior, elder son of Glov Senior, the best of company, and my friend. Colonel Krugel.

KRUGEL. Pleased to meet you.

OOTESH. Mr. Shonev.

SHONEV. Delighted, I'm sure.

OOTESH. Our host, Mr. Iharev.

IHAREV. Hi, Junior. Welcome to our home.

GLOV JUNIOR. Gentlemen, I . . . um . . . I . . . um . . .

OOTESH. Now don't stand on ceremony. Our motto is liberty—

KRUGEL. Equality.

SHONEV. *(who can't remember the next word).* And . . . what the hell?

KRUGEL. Fraternity.

SHONEV. Thank you, Colonel.

OOTESH. You agree, of course?

GLOV JUNIOR. What? Oh, oh, yes.

IHAREV. Bravo!

KRUGEL. Bravo!

SHONEV. Bravo!

OOTESH. Well done, good and faithful servant! Alexey, the champagne. *(ALEXEY pours champagne.)*

KRUGEL. Poverty?

OOTESH. No.

SHONEV. Chastity?

OOTESH. No-o-o. Can *you* help us, Mr. Iharev?

IHAREV. Courage. The courage of Mr. Glov Junior.

OOTESH. That's it. Very good. I know a poem about it. "O Courage . . ." or something. Who's holding the bank, me? Yes, a nice little bank of twenty thousand. *(Dealing.)* How much are *you* putting down, Krugel? *(The game begins.)* God moves in a mysterious way his wonders to perform. Well, the jack loses, the nine wins. Dark and inscrutable are the ways of fate. What? Win with a four? Now gentlemen, just watch that Ensign of Hussars. That Lieutenant, that Captain, that General, how he raises his stakes and the ace not out yet! Shonev, fill his glass for me, will you? He's creeping up on us . . . Oh, oh, here comes the ace, sweeping all before it like a typhoon in the sea of Marmora. Bravo. General Glov has won four thousand.

IHAREV. Bravo!

KRUGEL. Bravo!

SHONEV. Bravo!

GLOV JUNIOR. Double my stake!

OOTESH. Well done, General, well done. The seven leads, the seven . . . oh, oh, dear, the General has lost, too bad.

IHAREV. Too bad.

KRUGEL. Too bad.

SHONEV. Too bad.

OOTESH. Well, you can't win every time, my boy.

IHAREV. Better luck next time, my boy.

GLOV JUNIOR. Again! Again!

OOTESH. There we are, there we are, the General wins!

IHAREV. I give you Glov, General of Hussars!

KRUGEL. Hip hip . . .

SHONEV. Hooray!

KRUGEL. Hip hip . . .

SHONEV. Hooray!

KRUGEL. Hip hip . . .

SHONEV. Hooray!

OOTESH. The Queen of Spades. Shonev, remember that brunette we called the Queen of Spades? Where is she now? *(Tragically.)* Where is she now? You're right, Mr. Iharev: in the whorehouse downtown. Do you want the address? Uh huh, you lose, Krugel. You lose, Mr. Iharev. You lose, Shonev. General. I'm amazed, you lose.

GLOV JUNIOR. Damn it!

OOTESH. Did you hear that, Mr. Iharev? The man's a Hussar. He swears like a Hussar. Uh, huh, you lose again, General.

GLOV JUNIOR. Damn it, don't stop. How much in the bank?

OOTESH. Fifty thousand rubles. He swears like a real man. Like a Hussar. The whole fifty thousand, General?

IHAREV. The whole fifty thousand?

KRUGEL. The whole fifty thousand?

SHONEV. The whole fifty thousand?

OOTESH. Only a very great man would put all that down at once. I don't know if we have anyone as great as that left in the world. I don't know if . . .Uh, uh, he's a national hero, gentlemen: he's lost again.

GLOV JUNIOR. Don't stop! Don't stop! How much in the bank?

OOTESH. A hundred thousand rubles. You win, Krugel. You win, Mr. Iharev. You win, Shonev. The whole hundred thousand, general? Are you here incognito or something? Is your real name Napoleon Bonaparte? Look at his eyes, fellows, glowing like hot coals.

IHAREV. *De l'audace!*

KRUGEL. *De l'audace!*

SHONEV. *Et encore de l'audace!*

OOTESH. The primrose path to the everlasting bonfire . . .see?

IHAREV. General Glov is defeated yet again!

GLOV JUNIOR. Don't stop!

OOTESH. Just a minute, General. You've lost two hundred thousand. Before you bet again, you must pay up.

GLOV JUNIOR. Pay up?

IHAREV. Pay up!

KRUGEL. Pay up!

SHONEV. Pay up!

GLOV JUNIOR. Pay up? But I haven't got it.

OOTESH. It's easy.

KRUGEL. Just give us an I.O.U.

SHONEV. By coincidence Mr. Iharev has pen and ink ready.

GLOV JUNIOR. An I.O.U.

SHONEV. Just a little I.O.U.

OOTESH. And power of attorney to collect.

GLOV JUNIOR. Collect?

KRUGEL. From the bank.

IHAREV. Sign here.

GLOV JUNIOR *(signing)*. There! Now let's get back to the game.

KRUGEL. Now let's get back to the game.

SHONEV. Just one more thing.

OOTESH. Bring the money.

GLOV JUNIOR. What's the matter? You don't think you'll get paid?

KRUGEL. Money on the table.

GLOV JUNIOR. Don't be so goddamn mean. I . . .

OOTESH. We're not being goddamn mean.

KRUGEL. On the contrary.

SHONEV. We're being goddamn magnanimous.

OOTESH. A man who sits down without money can't lose.

KRUGEL. You're simply not playing the game, old man.

SHONEV. You're not playing the game.

GLOV JUNIOR. Fix any interest you like. I'll pay double.

OOTESH. Loan me some cash, fix any interest you like, *I'll* pay double.

GLOV JUNIOR. Will you play or won't you?

KRUGEL. We will.

SHONEV. We will.

OOTESH. If you bring the money.

GLOV JUNIOR *(taking out pistol).* Then good-bye forever! We shall meet in the next world. *(He rushes out.)*

OOTESH. I'll take care of this. *(He rushes out too.)*

IHAREV. There'll be hell to pay if the fool kills himself.

SHONEV. It'd be all right if he did it *after* handing the money over.

KRUGEL. But then the fool is a fool . . . *(Enter* OOTESH *dragging* GLOV JUNIOR.*)*

OOTESH. What do you think, gentlemen? He was standing there with this pistol in his handsome mouth.

KRUGEL. Ts, ts, ts.

IHAREV. Really. What next?

SHONEV. A Hussar—killing himself for a mere bagatelle?

IHAREV. Why, at that rate, everyone in Russia could kill himself.

KRUGEL. Which of us hasn't lost at cards?

SHONEV. Which of us isn't going to lose at cards?

GLOV JUNIOR. But I can't stand it!

IHAREV. Never say die! Chin up! Be a good loser!

OOTESH. He who wins, loses, he who loses wins. That's in the Bible.

GLOV JUNIOR. What does it mean?

KRUGEL. The loser wins.

SHONEV. You for instance.

OOTESH. An ensign that's lost two hundred thousand in one evening. Why, man, the Hussars will carry you on their shoulders.

GLOV JUNIOR. They will?

OOTESH. Why, of course they will.

KRUGEL. Of course they will.

SHONEV. *Absolument.*

OOTESH *(handing him a glass)*. Here, Ensign Glov.

GLOV JUNIOR. Three cheers for the Hussars!

IHAREV. Hip, hip . . .

ALL. Hooray!

KRUGEL. Hip, hip . . .

ALL. Hooray!

SHONEV. Hip, hip . . .

ALL. Hooray!

GLOV JUNIOR. I don't give a hoot in hell! Only what about father?

IHAREV. Father?

KRUGEL. Father?

SHONEV. Father?

GLOV JUNIOR. What shall I tell him?

OOTESH. Nothing.

KRUGEL. Not a thing!

GLOV JUNIOR. But he'll ask—the minute I cross the threshold.

KRUGEL. I have an idea.

OOTESH. So have I. Don't cross the threshold.

KRUGEL. Then he won't ask.

OOTESH. Go straight to your regiment.

KRUGEL. We'll provide the cash.

SHONEV. Ready cash somebody!

OOTESH. The ensign must enjoy himself before he leaves for the wars. Where's that girl with the black eyes?

GLOV JUNIOR. You saw her too? Yeah, where is she? I want to storm the fortress.

OOTESH *(to* KRUGEL*)*. Two hundred rubles for our Hussar.

KRUGEL *(to* SHONEV*)*. Two hundred rubles for our Hussar.

SHONEV *(to* IHAREV*)*. Two hundred rubles for our Hussar!

IHAREV *(paying up)*. Here!

GLOV JUNIOR. Thank you.

OOTESH. Thank you.

KRUGEL. Thank you.

SHONEV. Thank you.

GLOV JUNIOR. More champagne! Three cheers for the Hussars! Hip, hip . . .

OOTESH. One moment. I give you a toast. To true love. The love of a young Hussar and a simple peasant girl with coal black eyes. *(They drink.)*

GLOV JUNIOR. Three cheers for the Hussars! Hip, hip . . .

OOTESH. One moment. She's upstairs right now.

GLOV JUNIOR. The girl with the black eyes?

OOTESH. Wearing a dark green negligée and gold earrings.

GLOV JUNIOR. Well, gentlemen, I'm afraid I must be leaving.

OOTESH. We'll come with you, General.

GLOV JUNIOR. No please . . .

IHAREV. We'll come with you.

KRUGEL. We'll come with you.

SHONEV. We'll come with you.

GLOV JUNIOR. Please don't bother . . .

OOTESH. Isn't he a spark? The gay Lothario, eh?

GLOV JUNIOR. Well, good-bye, gentlemen. *(Exit GLOV JUNIOR.)*

OOTESH. Good-bye, Ensign.

IHAREV. Good-bye, Lieutenant.

KRUGEL. Good-bye, Captain.

SHONEV. Good-bye, General.

OOTESH *(still shouting after GLOV JUNIOR).* Don't forget to give us all details. See how it is, Iharev? We must treat him like Dresden china till we have the cash.

SHONEV. At that the bank might delay payment. I don't say they will. But they might.

KRUGEL. I'm very much afraid they might.

OOTESH. Business is business, even in a bank. Leave it to me. I shall oil their palms. *(There is a knock at the door.)* See who that is and tell him—tell him I'm in conference. *(KRUGEL goes to door with SHONEV. Enter CLERK.)*

CLERK. Excuse me. Oh, excuse me. I thought Mr. Glov Junior was here.

KRUGEL. Well, he's not.

SHONEV. He definitely is not.

KRUGEL. Mr. Glov Junior has just left.

SHONEV. Why?

CLERK. I've come to see him, gentlemen.

SHONEV. What for?

CLERK. On business.

OOTESH. Business? What's that? You couldn't be the man from the . . .

CLERK. Bank, sir.

OOTESH. Bank?

CLERK. The government bank.

OOTESH. Show the gentleman in, you fools. He's my best friend, Mr. Iharev. Come in, dear sir.

IHAREV. Come in, dear sir.

OOTESH. Pray be seated, dear sir.

IHAREV. Pray be seated, dear sir. A friend of Mr. Ootesh is a friend of mine.

OOTESH. We do business ourselves, dear sir.

KRUGEL. In fact we do business with Mr. Glov Junior, dear sir.

SHONEV. In fact it may be possible for you to create in us a fund of gratitude, dear sir.

CLERK. How can I do that?

OOTESH. Easy. Pay out that money this very minute.

CLERK. Oh, sir, I'm afraid it'd take a couple of weeks at the very least.

OOTESH. A couple of weeks?! You can't expect much gratitude for that.

CLERK. This is Russia, sir.

OOTESH. You agree, Mr. Iharev?

IHAREV. This is Russia.

CLERK. And a couple of weeks is Russian for a couple of months.

OOTESH. Yes, I can see that might be true for just Russians. We're more than just Russians, aren't we, Mr. Iharev?

IHAREV. We're friends.

KRUGEL. Of the family, you might say.

SHONEV. Bosom friends, as the saying goes.

OOTESH. Haven't I seen your face somewhere before?

CLERK. No, sir.

OOTESH. Don't contradict. I remember your name. Isn't it Fentifly Perpentitch?

CLERK. No, sir, it's Soy Stayhitch.

OOTESH. I never forget a name, Mr. Iharev. Or a face. What is more human than a face, Fentifly Perpentitch?

CLERK. Soy Stayhitch.

OOTESH. Don't change the subject. How's business?

CLERK. Sir, I'm a civil servant.

OOTESH. Then, how's tricks?

CLERK. Tricks, sir?

IHAREV. The tricks of the trade?

KRUGEL. Bribery and corruption?

SHONEV. You know . . . graft.

OOTESH. They mean, do you like working for the government? Ha! Ha! Ha!

CLERK. Oh. Oh, well. One has to live. Ha! ha! ha!

OOTESH. Hear that, Mr. Iharev? One has to live! Ha! ha! ha! *(General laugh, rising to a climax. Then sudden silence.)* Very well, Soy Stayhitch, we'll help you to live. *(Gives him a bribe.)* Now get going.

CLERK. The mills of God grind slowly.

OOTESH. Not when they're oiled with our money. Get moving!

CLERK. The mills of God . . . *(Exit CLERK.)*

OOTESH. If he's still talking about God I'd better give him three thousand right off. *(Exit OOTESH.)*

IHAREV. Three thousand. I've been thinking. Naturally we want the money as soon as possible, but on the other hand . . .

KRUGEL. Want it? We need it. We must have it.

SHONEV. If only we knew how to get round that bank clerk . . .

IHAREV. Now wait a minute. Why are you all in such a hell of a hurry? I can't . . . *(Enter* OOTESH.*)*

OOTESH. He can't do it in less than four days. I could choke.

IHAREV. Three days . . . four days. What difference does it make?

KRUGEL. A lot of difference.

SHONEV. A world of difference.

OOTESH. Didn't you know? Why, man, we must get to Nizny Novgorod.

IHAREV. Nizny Novgorod?

OOTESH. Nizny Novgorod. The merchants have all sent their sons to the market there to do business for them. Well, *you* know merchant's sons!

KRUGEL. Suckers!

SHONEV. Sissies!

OOTESH. Quite. We must get there at once!

KRUGEL. With a little capital in hand.

SHONEV. Say two hundred thousand.

IHAREV. I don't see how you can make it.

KRUGEL. I have an idea.

OOTESH. So have I.

SHONEV. I see what you mean.

OOTESH. You're not in a hurry, are you?

IHAREV. No.

OOTESH. Then you take Glov Junior's I.O.U.

IHAREV. Two hundred thousand rubles for me?

OOTESH. And let us have your eighty thousand.

IHAREV. What about the other hundred and twenty thousand?

OOTESH. We're in a jam. We'll have to pass it up.

IHAREV. Two hundred . . . All right. *(He hands over the money.)* Here's your eighty thousand.

OOTESH *(giving him I.O.U.).* Here's your two hundred thousand. Now I'll get Glov Junior and we'll regularize the whole deal. Krugel, take this money to our room. Here's the key to the cash box. *(Exit* KRUGEL.*)* Thanks, Iharev. Thanks to you, we'll be in Nizny Novgorod by sunrise! *(Exit* OOTESH.*)*

IHAREV. Yes, yes, don't waste any time on my account. Two hundred . . .

SHONEV. Let me give you a piece of advice. Don't stay here a moment longer than necessary. Come and join us. With two hundred thousand rubles you could buy the whole market. One second, I forgot to tell those fellows something. I'll be right back. *(Exit* SHONEV.*)*

IHAREV *(alone).* Two hundred thousand! In the morning I have eighty thousand rubles—in the evening, two hundred thousand. Why, some men would spend a lifetime putting that amount together. Twelve hours a day, six days a week, their hair turns grey, their teeth drop out, they get sick and die . . . whereas I . . . in one day . . . two hundred thousand rubles! How could you earn such money in these times? Even a country estate wouldn't yield that much, and who wants to waste a lifetime with yokels and hicks? A college graduate like me? Well, not a graduate exactly, but you know what I mean: Culture, self-improvement . . . If I want to go to Petersburg, I can go to Petersburg. Can't you just see me strolling down the English embankment there . . . in the summer gardens . . . in front of the Imperial Palace . . . "How are you, Countess?" . . . Going to the theatre in a carriage, *my* carriage. "Ivan, don't spare the horses, I want to catch the end of the second act." I'll go to Moscow too, dine at Yar's, wear the right clothes, hob-nob with . . . the arch duke, the arch duchess . . . "Now don't you be so arch, duchess" . . . and well, in general do my duty to Tsar and country. And to what do I owe my success? When they ask me what made me what I am today, so the little Russians of the future can go and do likewise, what shall I reply? Cheating at cards. "Of course, children, that's an over simplification. It's not cheating really. There should be another word. Maybe there *is* another word? A telling phrase? Business acumen? Success in business, my friends, is the reward of long years of service, not to mention innate business acumen." *(To the audience.)* Well, grant that it's cheating, how can you get along without? Huh? In a sense, it's merely, what shall I say? the self-preservation instinct. If I hadn't known how to cheat, they'd have cheated me, isn't that true? It was when they saw my . . . business acumen that they asked my assistance. You have to be smart. No, dedicated. That's the word. You have to be a dedicated man. To live foolishly, my friends, is easy, but to live wisely, with skill, finesse, subtlety, *savoir-faire, savoir-vivre, je ne sais quoi,* in other words, to cheat and not to be cheated, for that you have to be a dedicated man. *(GLOV JUNIOR rushes in.)*

GLOV JUNIOR. Where are they all? Their room's empty.

IHAREV. They stepped out for a minute.

GLOV JUNIOR. Out? With your money?

IHAREV. We made a deal. I stay on your account. *(Enter ALEXEY.)*

ALEXEY. You asked for the gentlemen, Mr. Glov?

GLOV JUNIOR. Yes.

ALEXEY. They've left.

GLOV JUNIOR. Left?

ALEXEY. Yes, their horses have been waiting outside for the past half hour.

GLOV JUNIOR. Oh sir, we're ruined.

IHAREV. Speak for yourself, Mr. Glov. With your two hundred thousand I shall be perfectly all right.

GLOV JUNIOR. What? My two hundred thousand?

IHAREV. Now calm down, young man. You're the loser. Get used to it.

GLOV JUNIOR. Don't you see you've been cheated?

IHAREV. What?

GLOV JUNIOR. Cheated!

IHAREV. That word! What are you talking about, Mr. Glov?

GLOV JUNIOR. What do you think's going on? You think my name is Glov? Do you think that old man . . . My name's not Glov. His name's not Glov. He's not my father. I'm not his son.

IHAREV. You're joking.

GLOV JUNIOR. Joking? Don't you see . . . I got cheated too! They didn't give me my cut.

IHAREV. You're hysterical, have a drink. What's all this about cuts and cheating? Do you think I am such a fool as . . . What about the bank? The power of attorney? Why, the clerk from the bank was here in this room. His name is Soy Stayhitch.

GLOV JUNIOR. No, it isn't. He's one of the gang too! His name is . . .

IHAREV. What? What??? *(Pause.)* Then who are you? *(Picks up stool.)* The devil himself come to plague me?

GLOV JUNIOR. Oh sir, they stripped me to the blast. When they'd finished with me I hadn't a shirt to my back. What could I do? They offered me three thousand to be Glov Junior. Haven't I come clean? I'm an honorable man, sir.

IHAREV. Honorable? Do you know what you are?

ALEXEY. If it's a fight, I blow. *(Exit ALEXEY.)*

IHAREV. You come with me!

GLOV JUNIOR. Where to, sir?

IHAREV. Where do you think, you crook? To the police station.

GLOV JUNIOR. Stop. Just for a minute. Please stop!

IHAREV. Well?

GLOV JUNIOR. Well, sir, I'd say you had no case.

IHAREV. No case? Why, it's highway robbery in broad daylight. Wait till I have you in the jail at Nerchinsk, I'll show you if I have a case or not!

GLOV JUNIOR. Yes, sir, that's very good, sir, but how about you, sir?

IHAREV. Me?

GLOV JUNIOR. You and your super-special decks of cards, sir?

IHAREV. Cards? Cards! He knows everything. It isn't fair. It just isn't fair.

GLOV JUNIOR. Never say die, sir.

IHAREV. What?

GLOV JUNIOR. Chin up! Be a good loser! Get used to it! And in moments of gloom, sir, when skies are grey, just say to yourself, there's always Adelaide. *(Exit GLOV JUNIOR.)*

IHAREV. To hell with Adelaide! *(He grabs Adelaide and flings her at the door. Queens and deuces fly to the floor.)* The scoundrels! The scoundrels!! Shame, shame, shame, upon them! *(He spits.)* It was a good job though, a clean job, a neat job!

Old Mr. Glov, young Mr. Glov, that bank clerk, and all in a
row, a beautiful performance. What a job, phew! And I can't
even sick the cops on them. It isn't fair. Mother always said,
you're smart, son, be yourself, and I was. I believed in cheating and I did cheat. I was a dedicated man. And where did it all
get me? Why, I might just as well have been stupid. I might
just as well . . . Gavrooshka! We're leaving! *(He puts on his
coat and hat and takes his cane.)* Yes, ladies and gentlemen, I'm
leaving, I've learned my lesson, and I'm leaving. I'm sure you
can take a hint. No? Well, let me put it this way. If you're
stupid, be yourself. If you're bright, try and be stupid. Try!
Good night.

APPENDIX A: Jan Kott on Gamblers

First published in Polish in 1962, translated for the present volume by Michael Kott, printed here by permission of Jan Kott.

The gambler is always an actor. Gambling is both acting and playing. The situation is given: it is the gambler's card hand. He must play within it. The swindler is an actor to the second power. He acts the part of the gambler, and, as the gambler, he must play his cards. The swindler also plays a third role: that of a decent and naive citizen, who was lured into the game. He is not just an actor: he is the director of the whole play. He chooses his cast as well as his characters; he even brings his own props. When swindlers plot, the group performance begins. The set is ready, the scenario prepared, and the plot has been invented. The characters are introduced and told to play their roles. The acting is to be realistic, or no one would be duped by the swindlers. The swindler plays the government official, the provincial judge, and the retired general. His fellow-traveler plays the prodigal son, the bribe-taker, and the rake. The third partner can play a *decent* swindler. The gambling house is the house of comedy. It could be a grand parable and a mirror. But for this we need a Gogol.

In *Gamblers* everyone is a swindler. All roles are played, even those of losers. This one-act play is faultless. The spectator is also cheated. He thought cheats did not cheat each other. He falls victim to a comedy staged by swindlers. Now he has to pay. The swindlers laugh last. Gogol's play is merciless. The gambling house turns into all of Russia. *Gamblers* is an instant picture of a quiet town far from Moscow. The play, like a funny mirror hung in a provincial inn, reflects the silhouettes of the guests, changing them into grotesque characters. This mirror is the *Theatrum Mundi*.

Game is a crucial theme for the modern grotesque. The situation not only limits the gambler: it dictates the opening move to him. The actor plays himself and his part. But all the parts are cast in advance; the actor's character is also a role. The philosophy of this playlet is unexpected and rancorous.

THE MARRIAGE

While the Constance Garnett translation will remain necessary for those who wish to know, line by line, what Gogol wrote, if Gogol's plays are to find readers and producers today it seems desirable to take greater liberties with the material. The Bentley version is an attempt to re-create Gogol's vivacity rather than to reproduce his phraseology. It is not to be expected that such a treatment will give pleasure to those who have access to the original; it is directed to those who have not. To translate a funny line with an unfunny line can hardly be described as fidelity to a text; yet, in order to translate a funny line with another funny line, the translator usually has to invent something of his own. The story of *The Marriage,* an example of Gogol's unsurpassed narrative art, has been tampered with in only one particular. In the original, the merchant Starikov appears on stage among the other suitors. For an audience that can infer everything from such a man's dress and accent, his brief appearance has presumably some value. For the Anglo-American audience it has none. Starikov has therefore been removed from the cast of characters, though his place in the scheme of things is made clear in the speeches of Aunt Arina: her speeches, except the last part of the last one, are taken without significant change from the Russian. With this one small exception, the structure of Gogol's play remains intact. The sequence of scenes remains what he made it. No character has been deliberately changed. Nothing in Gogol's method has been rejected as old-fashioned: the asides appear here almost exactly as in the Russian. Changes were made only when the English dialogue lacked vitality without them. The adapter began with a complete and literal text but soon realized that if his final script was to be continuously comic many a lifeless phrase would have to be cut and not a few lively phrases added. Russia is a long way off, and so are the Eighteen Thirties: one cannot transport plays from that stage to ours without acknowledging and trying to solve the problems glanced at here.

FROM A MADMAN'S DIARY

This text differs from the other three in this book in being abridged, streamlined. Why? A masterpiece is a masterpiece, to tamper is to spoil, to shorten is to remove something the master considered pertinent and integral. The adapter's excuse is that *The Madman's Diary* is not a play but a story. For reading in a book, the length *is* exactly right, every word adds, Gogol's judgment was perfect. The aim here is adaptation to the stage, hence to English spoken out loud and projected in a theatre. The present adapter is not under the illusion that, even in the theatre, shorter is always better than longer, faster always better than slower. He does believe, though, that the conditions of theatre are to a degree peculiar, that theatre art has its own exactions. A rhythm which may be acceptable at home in an armchair can prove unacceptable from an orchestra seat, and while a reading at home may be discontinued and resumed later, a seeing-and-hearing in the theatre has to be a single uninterrupted "trip" describing, as it were, a parabola in the air, with its beginning, its high point, and its rounding off. The adapter hunted for the right length—the length of *A Madman's Diary* when offered as a single, uninterrupted experience in a theatre. Brevity as such was not sought. No number of minutes was fixed in advance as the amount of time to be allotted as with a TV program. The little show might have turned out even shorter. Or longer: heaven knows, many superb details are omitted—they would have been included if it had seemed that their inclusion would enhance the drama. Decisive was the overall impression of listening to it. It had to move along at the right pace and with the most powerful dynamics. It had to strike home with the maximum impact. It had to end right. At the cost of a certain immodesty, the adapter would like to add that there is sometimes something to be said for abridgment after all, particularly abridgment of a very great classic, perfect though it may be as it stands. Jean Cocteau even made a short version of Sophocles *Antigone,* describing as follows the principle that guided him:

> It is very tempting to photograph Greece from the air. We find it then has a fresh, a new appearance . . . With a bird's eye view, some great beauties disappear, but others arise. Unexpected associations, blocks, shadows, angles and contrasts are discovered.

GAMBLERS

However the Russian original may read to Russians, a literal translation into English reads quite badly. The language is apt to seem like fleshy tissue, and the imperative imposes itself to cut the prose to the bone. The changes which automatically result from this process exact from the adapter some further, non-automatic changes; for, in its new and admittedly attenuated form, the dialogue must at all costs have the pace of farce, the tone of frivolity, hence the presence in the Bentley version of many lines that Gogol did not write. He referred to no civil war or higher mystery; could scarcely, in the Russia of Nicholas I (whom anyway he admired) have brought up liberty, equality, and fraternity; and did not attribute to Hussars a white uniform and giant epaulets. Possibly some of these inventions are too extravagant, but then too Gogol was the most extravagant of men. There are also questions of language. How informal can the tone become, how slangy, how vulgar? Some people may feel that the dialogue should not shuttle between the Old World formal "Much obliged, I'm sure," and the New World jocular "Okay, pal," yet just such shuttling is familiar to vaudeville fans, and it is easy to imagine Groucho Marx delivering himself of either expression. In the original, Ootesh is called Uteshitelny. Re-instate this by all means, reader, if you can stand it—if you can even say it. Alternatively, you could translate the name. It means Mr. Comforting or Mr. Re-assuring, but one fears that such a name, in English, might suggest *Pilgrim's Progress* rather than low comedy; yet it is worth a mention here, perhaps, as indicating that Ootesh is a Soapy Sam. The form Ootesh is ridiculous, of course: let it be ridiculous. The first American production of this script, and perhaps of Gogol's play in any form, took place under the direction of the adapter at the Herbert Berghof Studio, New York City, in 1955. The present text was worked out in that production, and in one that followed it that same year at Crystal Lake Lodge in upstate New York, producer: Howard Da Silva (Morris Carnovsky as Ootesh, Martin Waldron as Iharev). Among the liberties that crept into the text during rehearsals was a certain redistribution of lines among the gang. Some of Ootesh's lines were given to Shonev and Krugel who otherwise, we found, would too often have been left out in the cold, and further echoing sequences were included on the lines of:

OOTESH. It's a small world.
SHONEV. Tiny.
KRUGEL. Infinitesimal.

As with Starikov in *The Marriage,* one often has the feeling with minor characters in *Gamblers* that while their mere appearance may mean something to a Russian audience it means nothing to an American one. The adapter confesses being unable to hold a mirror to the Krugel and Shonev of Gogol and, in his impotence, he made them over into a traditional comedy team (Krugel heavy and clumsy, Shonev delicate and whimsical), talking according to a definite formula. It is an archetypal comic coupling, Sir Toby Belch and Sir Andrew Aguecheek.

INSPECTOR

(This note comes last because the English version was the last to be made.)

There is less to be said here about this play, either because the principles involved have already been stated, or because fewer liberties were taken with the text. The only sizable omissions are cited in footnotes to that text.

I was tempted to use the one-word Russian title *Revizor* but settled for a one-word title, never perhaps used hitherto for the play in English, *Inspector.*

What such an Inspector is cannot be clear unless the audience knows what his antagonist is. Most English translations (more than a dozen have been printed) call him the Mayor. I find Governor somewhat less misleading, but *any* English rendering will benefit from an elaboration compactly given with the Seymour-Noyes translation:

> The office of gorodnichy [this is the Russian word translated as Mayor or Governor], or chief of city police, existed from 1775 to 1862. The gorodnichy was appointed by the imperial authorities in Petersburg and was responsible to them. His duties were far more extensive than those of the chief of police of an American or an English city.

An experience of the translator's may be worth reporting. In my first draft I tried to enliven the dialogue by modernization—business community, for instance, for "shopkeepers." It did not work. Just as the gorodnichy is not an English or American mayor, so the despised shopkeepers of provincial Russia in the Eighteen Thirties are not your modern Rotary Club or even your old-fashioned Elks. Whatever universal truths Gogol has to offer will come through better if the specific facts of Russia in the Eighteen Thirties are presented to the ear and eye.

Many characters, in a tradition we know from Ben Jonson and Dickens, have names that mean things. Some translator, one day, will use English equivalents along the following lines. (Not all the Russian names appear in my version, titles [like "the Judge"] being so much easier to remember.) The following list is taken from *Masterpieces of Russian Drama* edited by George Rapall Noyes.

Skvoznik-Dmukhanovsky	Rascal-Puftup
Hlopov	Bedbug
Lyapkin-Tyapkin	Bungle-Steal
Zemlyanika	Strawberry
Hlestakov	Whipper Snapper
Lyulykov	Halloo
Rastakovsky	Say Yes
Korobkin	Blockhead
Ukhovertov	Earwig
Svistunov	Whistle
Pugovitzin	Buttons
Derzhimorda	Hold Your Face
Abdulin	Tartar
Poshlepkin	Draggletail

APPENDIX C: What to read next by and about Gogol

In the Russian edition of the works, published over the period 1937-1952 in Moscow, there are fourteen sizable volumes. Much of this material has still not been translated in English. Those who have no Russian but can read French or German can fill in some of their Gogol gaps in these latter languages. Attention is confined here to English-language versions. Currently, the most widely-read translation of *Dead Souls* is by Andrew R. MacAndrew (Signet Classics). New translations of *Inspector* are published all the time, which is why none should be listed here as the latest. The same goes for miscellaneous collections of Gogol stories. The *collected* stories are another matter. It would seem that only Constance Garnett ever essayed them, and one must be grateful that the University of Chicago Press has re-issued the Garnett version, as revised by Leonard J. Kent, in 1985.

About the plays as a group. When I was sixteen, I received a copy of *The Government Inspector and Other Plays,* from the Russian by Constance Garnett. Since I knew many passages by heart before I learned a word of Russian, it is obvious that, in a very intimate way, Mrs. Garnett's versions underlie and underpin my own. Indeed there seems to have been no other English-language edition of the plays as a group until long after the bulk of this present volume was prepared, namely, until the University of Chicago Press issued *The Theater of Nikolay Gogol* in 1980, edited with introduction and notes by Milton Ehre, translated by Milton Ehre and Fruma Gottschalk.

Outside of the stories and plays, the following three volumes are notable:

Divine Liturgy of the Eastern Church. London, 1960.

Letters of Nikolai Gogol, selected and edited by Carl R. Proffer. Ann Arbor, Michigan, 1967.

Selected Passages from Correspondence with Friends, translated by Jesse Zeldin. Nashville, Tennessee, 1968.

Supplementary to the plays, certain periodical and other material has relevance, notably:

The notes and selections contained in the Milton Ehre volume listed above.
Gogol's "After the Play." Tulane Drama Review, Winter, 1959.

ABOUT GOGOL

At least six books written in English are worth mentioning here:

1. Nabokov, Vladimir: Nikolai Gogol. Norfolk, Connecticut, 1944.
2. Magarshack, David: Gogol, a Life. New York, 1957.
3. Debreczeny, Paul: Nikolai Gogol and his Contemporary Critics. Philadelphia, Pennsylvania, 1966.
4. Erlich, Victor: Gogol. New Haven, Connecticut, 1969.
5. Karlinsky, Simon: The Sexual Labyrinth of Nikolai Gogol. Cambridge, Massachusetts, 1976.
6. Worrall, Nick: Nikolai Gogol and Ivan Turgenev. London, 1982.

Among translations into English, three books might be noted:

1. Setchkarev, V.: Gogol, His Life and Works. New York, 1965.
2. Troyat, Henri: Divided Soul, the Life of Gogol. New York, 1973.
3. Maguire, Robert A., ed., Gogol from the 20th Century. Princeton, New Jersey, 1973.

Otherwise the notable comments on Gogol in English have been those of various writers in scattered essays and reviews. The best that have come to the present editor's attention are these six:

1. Kott, Jan: "The Eating of the Government Inspector," in Theatre Quarterly (London), March-May 1975. (Reprinted in Kott's book Theatre of Essence. Evanston, Illinois, 1985.)

2. O'Connor, Frank: "Foreword" to the MacAndrew translation of *Dead Souls* as cited above.

3. Pritchett, V. S.: "The Open Imagination," in The New Statesman and Nation, February 2, 1957.

4. Rahv, Philip: "Gogol as a Modern Instance," a talk given at Columbia University in 1952, and printed in the 2nd edition of the author's Image and Idea, Norfolk, Conn., 1957.

5. Wilson, Edmund: "Gogol: the Demon in the Overgrown Garden," in The Nation, December 6, 1952.

6. Worrall, Nick: "Meyerhold Directs Gogol's *Government Inspector*," Theatre Quarterly, July-September 1972.

No reading list in this field would be complete without a mention of D. S. Mirsky's History of Russian Literature, first published by Knopf in 1926-7.

DRAMATIC REPERTOIRE

THE CLASSIC THEATRE And
World's Great Drama For the American Stage.

THE SERVANT OF TWO MASTERS and
Other Italian Classics
Edited by Eric Bentley

THE SERVANT OF TWO MASTERS Goldoni
English Version by Edward Dent

THE KING STAG Gozzi
English Version by Carl Wildman

THE MANDRAKE Machiavelli
English Version by Frederick May and
Eric Bentley

RUZZANTE RETURNS FROM THE WARS
Beolco
English Version by Angela Ingold and Theodore
Hoffman

ISBN: 0-936839-20-1

272 pages, 5½ x 8¼, Notes

BEFORE BRECHT: Four German Plays
Edited and Translated by Eric Bentley

LEONCE AND LENA by Georg Buchner

LA RONDE by Arthur Schnitzler

SPRING AWAKENING by Frank Wedekind

UNDERPANTS by Carl Sternheim

ISBN: 0-87910-229-2
272 pages, 5½ x 8¼, Notes

3 GREAT JEWISH PLAYS

"All the plays in this volume have intrinsic merit. These are "classics" reflecting the essential Jewish view of life ... Yet if the book contained nothing else, the introduction by Joseph Landis would make it worth preserving. Landis gives us what is virtually a summation of the Jewish world view."

—Harold Clurman

EDITED AND IN MODERN TRANSLATIONS BY
JOSEPH C. LANDIS
OUTSTANDING DRAMA BY
LEIVICK • ANSKI • ASCH

THE DYBBUK by S. Anski
The most famous of all Yiddish plays, THE DYBBUK has enjoyed thousands of performances since Stanislavski took up its cause in 1914.

THE GOLEM by H. Leivick
A masterpiece of poetic drama, THE GOLEM presents a powerful metaphor of the Jewish aversion to violence and brute force as a means to even the most compelling ends.

GOD OF VENGEANCE by Sholem Asch
Bold, theatrical triumph around the world, towering talents such as Rudolph Schildkraut and David Kessler have made the play and its protagonist Chapchovich, unforgettable experiences in the Yiddish theatre.

272 PAGES, 5½ × 8¼
ISBN: 0-936839-04-X

APPLAUSE
THEATRE BOOK PUBLISHERS

The Brute and Other Farces
by Anton Chekhov
Edited by Eric Bentley

"INDISPENSABLE!"

—*Robert Brustein*
Director, Loeb Drama
Center
Harvard University

The blustering, stuttering eloquence of Chekhov's unlikely heroes has endured to shape the voice of contemporary theatre. This volume presents seven minor masterpieces:

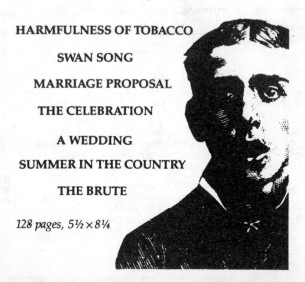

HARMFULNESS OF TOBACCO

SWAN SONG

MARRIAGE PROPOSAL

THE CELEBRATION

A WEDDING

SUMMER IN THE COUNTRY

THE BRUTE

128 pages, 5½ × 8¼